iPhone
User Guide

The Comprehensive Step-by-Step
Instruction and Illustrated Manual for
Beginners & Seniors to Master the
iPhone 16 Pro with Tips and Tricks for
iOS 18

Shawn Blaine

Table of Contents

Introduction

Welcome to the "iPhone 16 Pro User Manual." Before we delve into the tips, tricks, and setup, let's quickly review the device's features. Let's quickly go over the features of the device.

The iPhone 16 Pro screen is now bigger thanks to the 6.3-inch screen size. It comes with iOS 18, a large battery capacity, a camera control button, a revamped 48-megapixel main "Fusion" sensor, up to 1 TB of storage, and Apple Intelligence, which powers many features in the phone. Apple has also retained the Ceramic Shield to protect the device's body.

Staring at the right corner of the iPhone, you will see the new Camera Control key. It allows you to quickly launch the camera and shoot videos or photos. You can also use it to move to different settings or swipe and tap a menu on the iPhone.

Apple has equipped the iPhone 16 Pro and the rest in the series with the A18 Pro chip, which offers more speed and performance than the previous chipset.

The new chip has propelled the integration of Apple Intelligence, which brings artificial intelligence features to the iPhone.

Apple has rebranded the main camera to "Fusion Camera." It boasts a 2x in-sensor zoom, an ultrawide 48-megapixel resolution, and a 5x zoom for the telephoto camera.

There's a new Cinematic Slow-Motion mode that takes video recording to another dimension.

In addition, Apple has improved its photographic styles, which are built-in effects that apply to particular colors, so you may change the mood of your photos just by adjusting the colors. They're also more adaptable, thanks to a new control pad that lets you adjust the hue and saturation to your liking.

This introduction only scratches the surface of the iPhone 16 Pro's capabilities, and with iOS 18, you'll uncover new features and learn how to utilize them in this guide. Without further ado, let's start with setting up the device for the first time.

Chapter One

Setting up iPhone

Once you've charged the iPhone, you can start setting up your preferences to maximize the phone's features.

- Long-tap the Side key, which is located on the device's top right corner.
- Then, the "**Hello**" menu will pop up. Swiping up, select your preferred language and country.
- Hit on "**Continue**."
- On the "**Quick Start**" window, press the "**Set Up Without Another Device**" option. If you own an older iPhone, you can immediately sign into the new iPhone by following the onscreen instructions in the Quick Start window.

- You'll be shown the Wi-Fi window; follow up by selecting a Wi-Fi network; and insert the Wi-Fi password. After that, press "**Join**." If you'd rather activate your device through a network carrier, then touch "**Use Cellular Connection**."
- After reviewing the "**Data & Privacy**" window, touch "**Continue**."

- Once the "**Set Up iPhone**" pops up, press the "**Set Up for Myself**" option if you're setting up the phone for yourself.

- Follow up by clicking "**Continue**." Once you get to the window that asks to set up Face ID, press "**Continue**." Proceed according to the instructions.
- If you prefer to activate Face ID later, then press "**Set Up Later**."
- Next, you'll see the Passcode window, follow up by inserting a six-digit

passcode, then repeat to validate. In order to change the passcode type, hit on "**Passcode Options**."

- If you need to import apps and data onto your iPhone while on the "**Transfer your App & Data**" window, go ahead and select your preferred method. To skip, touch the "**Don't Transfer Anything**" button.
- Continue by entering your Apple ID and password. Follow this by clicking "Next." Select " **Forgot password or Don't have an Apple ID?**" to proceed with creating one. After that, press "**Agree**." Next up, press "**Continue**."
- You may toggle "**Location Services**" and other features on or off by pressing the corresponding button.
- Press "**Continue**" and follow the on-screen instructions to set up Apple Pay. To postpone the setup, touch "**Set Up Later in Wallet**."
- Then, press "**Continue**."
- Then, to set up Siri, follow the on-screen instructions. Choose "**Set Up Later in Settings**" to postpone the Siri setup.
- Then, follow the on-screen instructions to configure the other functionality.
- Swipe up to access your phone's home screen when you reach the last screen of the setup menu.

Turn on iPhone

If your iPhone is off and you need to power it on, simply long-tap the side button until the Apple logo shows up on the screen, then let go.

Turn Off iPhone

You can also power off your phone through the buttons and the Shut Down menu in the Settings app.

Use Hardware Buttons

- Long-tap the side and volume up button simultaneously to show the power off menu.

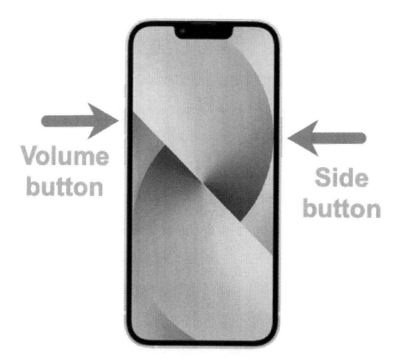

- Proceed by sliding the "**slide to power off**" slider towards the right.

Use Power Button

- Move to the Settings app.
- From there, hit "**General**."
- After that, press "**Shut Down**."

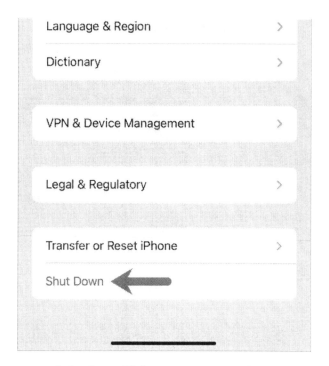

- Slide the "**slide to power off**" towards the right.

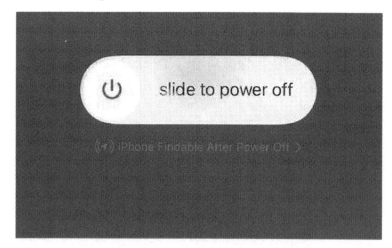

Use Control Center

There's a new method to power off your iPhone.

- Swipe downward from the upper right edge of the home screen.
- Press the Power button at the upper right.

- Finish up by swiping the power slider to the right.

Force Restart iPhone

If your phone's screen suddenly becomes unresponsive, you can use force restart to make the issue go away.

- Begin by pressing the volume up button, then let go.
- Then tap the volume down button.
- Proceed by long-tapping the side button until the Apple icon shows up.

Download New iOS

Once a new iOS becomes available, you can have it installed on your phone.

- Move to the Settings app.
- Afterward, select "**General**."
- From there, hit "**Software Update**."
- If there are multiple updates, select your preferred option.
- After that, select "**Install Now**." However, if the "**Download and Install**" button is what you see, click on it, then input your passcode and choose the "**Install Now**" option.

Automatic iOS Updates

You may want these new updates to install automatically.

- Launch the Settings app.
- Click on "**General**."
- Then hit on "**Software Update**."
- From there, hit "**Automatic Updates**."
- Ensure you activate the two "**iOS Updates**" toggle.

Deactivate Optimized Battery Charging

Once you enable Optimized Battery Charging, your iPhone will stop charging when the battery reaches 80%. This is to ensure that your battery doesn't wear off quickly and helps to enhance the battery's life span.

- Launch the Settings app.
- Move down and select "**Battery**."

- From there, select "**Charging Optimization**."

- Follow up by selecting "**None**" or "**80% Limit**."

- If you choose the later, your phone will stop charging once it gets to 80%.

Wake your iPhone

To conserve power and prevent unwanted access, the iPhone screen dims and shuts down. You can wake it up and start using it again. Here are three methods you can use.

- Press the side key.

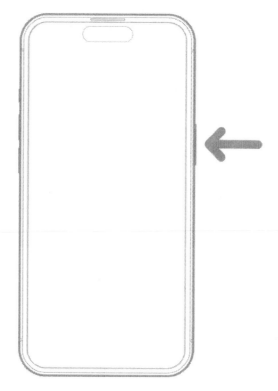

- Raise the iPhone.

- Click on the iPhone display.

Connect to a Wi-Fi Network

If you'd prefer not to use your mobile data, you can access and surf the internet using Wi-Fi.

- Head to the Settings app.
- Next, select "**Wi-Fi**."

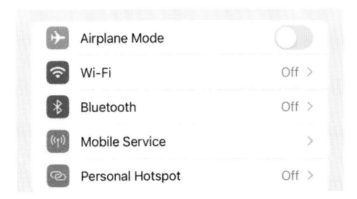

- Follow up by enabling the "**Wi-Fi**" switch to the on position.

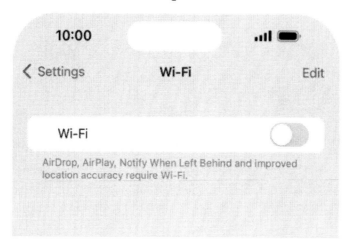

- Select an available Wi-Fi network
- Insert the password, then select "**Join**." This will automatically pair your iPhone with the network.

To manually pair:

- Select "**Other**."
- Follow up by inserting the required network name.
- From there, select "**Security**."

- Pick the security type (WPA, WEP, and more).
- After that, select "**Other Network**."
- Follow up by inserting the password, then select "**Join**."

Delete a Wi-Fi Connection

You can disconnect your phone from a Wi-Fi.

- Head to the Settings app.
- Next up, select "**Wi-Fi**."

- After this, select the Info sign .
- From there, select "**Forget this Network**."
- Lastly, select "**Forget**."

Extend your Battery Life

Certain applications that demand a lot of power will drastically reduce your phone's battery life. By activating the low power mode, you'll be able to minimize the power consumption.

- Head to the Settings app.
- From there, select "**Battery**."

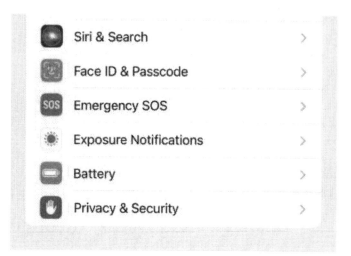

- Hit the switch next to "**Low Power Mode**" to toggle it on/off.

Activate Apple ID

Apple ID gives you access to services like iTunes, iCloud, and more. While setting up your iPhone for the first time, there's always a prompt to set up an Apple ID. If you missed it, follow these steps.

- Head to the Settings app.
- From there, touch "**Sign in to your iPhone.**"

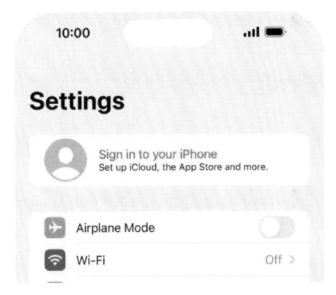

- If you've previously created an account, insert your credentials to sign in.
- If you've never set it up before, touch "**Don't have an Apple ID?**" Go through the prompts to create one.

Apple ID

Sign in with an email or phone number to use iCloud, the App Store, Messages or other Apple services.

Email or Phone Number

Don't have an Apple ID?

Forgot Password?

- Follow up by inserting your Email or Phone Number inside the provided text field.
- Then select "**Continue.**"
- Insert a password in the provided text field, then select "**Continue.**"

Switch Apple ID

You can log out of your Apple ID.

- Move to the Settings app.
- Touch the profile at the top.
- Move down, then touch "**Sign Out.**"
- Insert your Apple ID password.
- From there, touch "**Turn Off**" at the upper right.

- Follow up by toggling on or off the desired options.
- Lastly, select "**Sign Out**."

Add Two-Factor Authentication

Two-factor authentication offers an additional security net to ensure that another person doesn't sign into your Apple ID account. Your phone number or email will automatically receive a verification code when you attempt to log in.

- Move to the Settings app.
- Touch the Apple ID at the top.
- From there, touch "**Sign-In & Security**."
- Follow up by selecting "**Turn On Two-Factor Authentication**."
- After that, touch "**Continue**."
- Go through the prompts.

Enable Mobile Data

To utilize mobile data for internet browsing, follow these steps:

- Move to the Settings app.
- After that, select "**Mobile Service**."

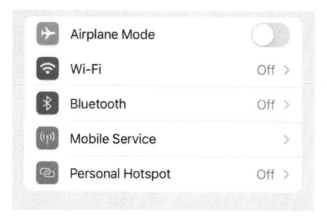

- Follow up by pressing the switch next to "**Mobile Data**" to the on/off position.

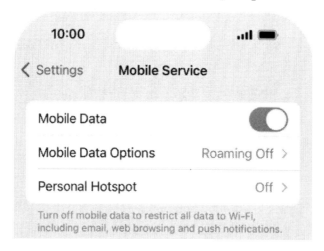

- Continue by pressing the switch next to the listed applications to enable or disable them.

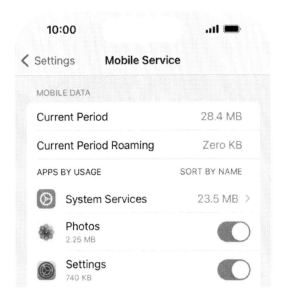

Chapter Two

Enable iCloud Backup

If you activate iCloud backup, Apple will store a copy of your phone files on their server, allowing you to recover them in the event of damage or loss.

- Launch the Settings app.
- Select the profile at the top.
- From there, hit "**iCloud**."

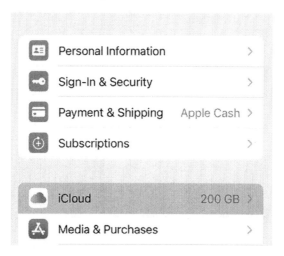

- Up next, press "**iCloud Backup**."
- Click on **Backup Now**" to instantly initiate the back up.
- For automatic backup, ensure you toggle on the "**Backup This iPhone**" switch.

Erase Data

You can wipe off all the files on your phone if you wish to gift it to someone. Ensure you've backed up your files before doing that.

- Launch the Settings app.
- From there, hit "**General.**"
- Up next, touch "**Transfer or Reset iPhone.**"

- From there, touch "**Erase All Content and Settings**."

- Go through the onscreen guideline.

Restore your Backup

After erasing your files, you can retrieve it when setting up another iPhone.

- Long-tap your phone side button to power it on.
- Swipe upward on the "**Hello**" menu to select a language.
- Follow the prompts.
- Once you arrive at the "**Apps & Data**" menu, hit on "**Restore from iCloud Backup**."
- Go through the prompts to complete.

Set up iCloud Plus

iCloud Plus grants you access to more storage space and other features such as Hide My Email, etc.

- Move to the Settings app.
- Select your Apple ID from the top.

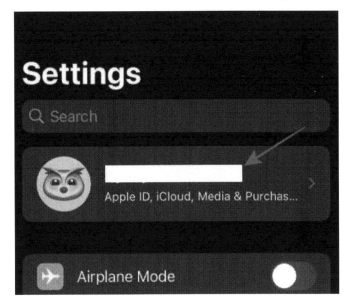

- From there, hit "**iCloud**."

- Up next, touch "**Manage Storage**."

- After that, hit "**Change Storage Plan**."

- Proceed by selecting your desired plan.

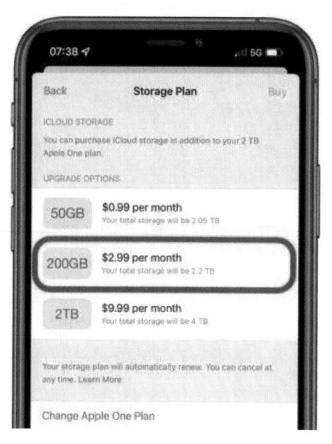

- Go through the prompts to purchase the selected option.

Enable iCloud Private Relay

Thanks to iCloud Private Relay, your location will be masked when you're surfing the internet making it difficult to be tracked.

- Move to the Settings app.
- Select your Apple profile at the upper menu.
- Up next, hit "**iCloud**."

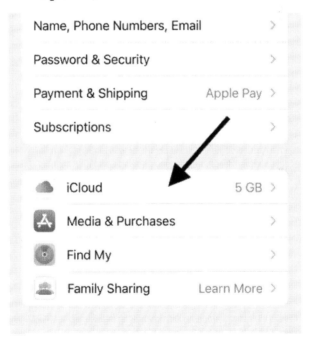

- From there, touch "**Private Relay**."

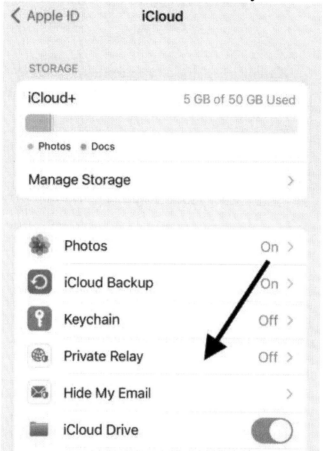

- Touch the switch next to "**Private Relay**" to activate it.
- After that, press "**IP Address Location**."
- Then select any of the option.

Hide My Email

Even though some people would rather not give out their information online, the vast majority of services still demand an email address from new customers. "Hide My Email" creates a dummy email address for you, but redirects all incoming messages to your real mailbox. When signing up for websites, you'll enter the dummy email address. Ensure you're subscribed to iCloud Plus to have access to this feature.

Turn on Hide My Email

- Launch the Settings app.
- Select your Apple profile from the upper menu.
- Up next, hit "**iCloud**."

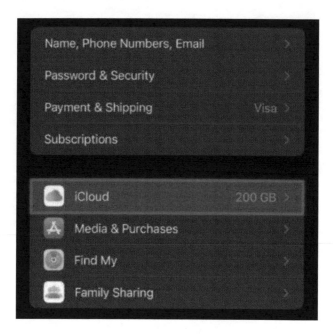

- From there, touch **"Hide My Email."**

- Thereafter, touch "**Create New Address**."
- A random dummy email address will be created for you. Hit on the "**Use different address**" to generate another if you don't fancy the first option. Otherwise, choose "**Continue**."

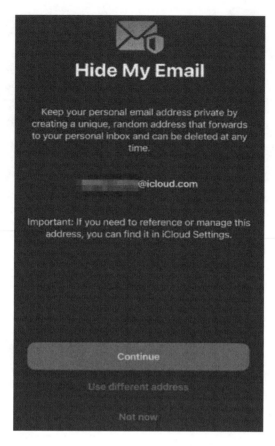

- Go through the prompts to finish it.

Disable Hide My Email Address

- Launch the Settings app.
- Select your Apple profile from the upper menu.
- Up next, hit "**iCloud**."
- After which, touch "**Hide My Email**."

- Locate the dummy email addresses you wish to deactivate.
- From there, touch "**Deactivate email address**."
- Thereafter, hit on "**Deactivate**."

Using Hide My Email in Safari

When filling out online form and wish to use Hide My Email, then do this:

- Move to the Safari app and input the URL.
- Select the email field when asked.
- Then select the "**Hide My Email**" button that appears above your keyboard. A newly generated dummy address will pop up. If you dislike it, hit the Refresh icon ↻ to generate a new one.
- Then touch "**Continue**" to utilize the suggested address.
- Hit on "**Continue**."

Set up Email

People that uses email providers such as Yahoo, Google, iCloud and other popular ones can automatically add their email in the Settings app.

- Move to the Settings app.
- In there, touch "**Mail**."
- Afterward, press "**Accounts**."

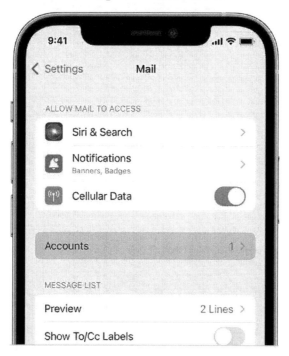

- From there, touch "**Add Account**."
- Follow up by choosing your email provider.

- After that, select "**Next**."
- Follow the prompts, then hit "**Save**."

You can still manually add other less popular email service.

- Launch the Settings app.
- Click on "**Mail**."
- Thereafter, touch "**Accounts**."
- From there, touch "**Add Account**."
- Up next, select "**Other**."
- After which, hit "**Add Mail Account**."
- Follow up by inserting your information and account description.
- Then select "**Next**."
- Hold on while Mail locates the email settings and complete the process.
- Once finished, touch "**Done**."

Set up Face ID

Face ID can be used to authenticate payment, unlock your phone and protect its content from prying eyes.

- Move to the Settings app.
- After that, touch "**Face ID & Passcode**." Input your passcode if asked.

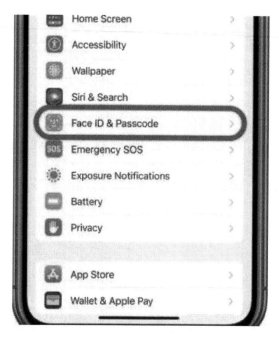

- From there, touch "**Set Up Face ID**."
- Position your face to appear within the camera frame.
- Then hit "**Get Started**."

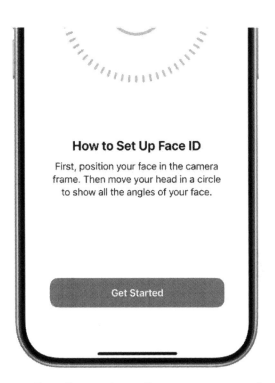

How to Set Up Face ID

First, position your face in the camera
frame. Then move your head in a circle
to show all the angles of your face.

Get Started

- Select "**Continue**" once you complete
  the first scan.
- Follow up by moving your head to
  complete the second scan.
- Then select "**Done**."

Disable Face ID

- Move to the Settings app.
- After that, touch "**Face ID &
  Passcode**." Input your passcode if
  asked.

- Touch the switch beside the "**Reset Face ID**."

Set up Passcode

You can also add a Passcode to secure your phone.

- Launch the Settings app.
- From there, touch "**Face ID & Passcode**."
- After this, touch "**Turn Passcode On**."

- Go ahead and insert your preferred 6-digit passcode. To explore other passcode type, press "**Passcode Options**."

Change Passcode

You can choose a new passcode if the old one has been compromised.

- Launch the Settings app.
- Thereafter, touch "**Face ID & Passcode**."
- Follow up by inserting your current passcode if asked
- After which, hit "**Change Passcode**."
- Follow the prompts.

Disable Passcode

You can deactivate your passcode when needed.

- Launch the Settings app.
- From there, touch "**Face ID & Passcode**."
- Thereafter, hit on "**Turn Passcode Off**."

Disable Attention Awareness

Attention Awareness ensures that your phone screen doesn't dim when you're staring at it. You can deactivate it if needed.

- Move to the Settings app.
- From there, touch "**Face ID & Passcode**."
- Press the switch beside the "**Attention Aware Features**" option to deactivate it.

Chapter Three

Enable Apple Pay

You'll be able to pay for your online and physical store purchases by setting up Apple Pay without having to carry your credit card everywhere you go. The Wallet application saves your card and uses it for future purchases once you've added it.

- Head to the Wallet app.
- From there, touch the + icon.

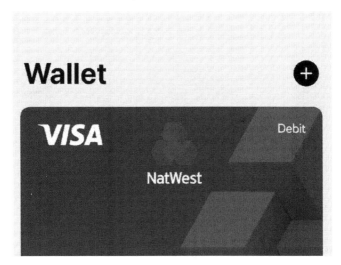

- Next up, press "**Debit or Credit Card**."

Add to Wallet

Keep all the cards, keys and passes you use every day all in one place.

Available Cards

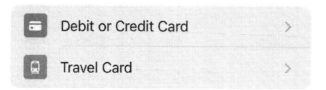

| | Debit or Credit Card | > |
| | Travel Card | > |

- After that, select "**Continue**."

- Follow up by positioning the credit card so that it the details are automatically captured by your phone's camera.
- Then, select "**Next**."
- Following this, insert your card's CVV and touch "**Next**."

❮ Back   Next

Card Details

Verify and complete your card information.

Expiry Date

Security Code

- After this, select "**Agree**."

prompted to accept or reject any material change to this Agreement the next time you use the Service after COMMUNITY 1ST CREDIT UNION has made the change. Your acceptance of the revised terms and conditions along with the continued use of the Services will indicate your consent to be bound by the revised Agreement. Further, COMMUNITY 1ST CREDIT UNION reserves the right, in its sole discretion, to change, modify, add, or remove portions from the Services. Your continued use of the Services will indicate your acceptance of any such changes to the Services.

2. Limitations of Service. When using the Services, you may experience technical or other difficulties. We will attempt to post alerts on our website or send you a text message to notify you of these

Disagree   Agree

- Thereafter, press "**Next**."
- Follow the prompts to finish the procedure.
- You'll see the Apple icon on stores that accepts Apple Pay. Once you've followed the above steps and linked your card with Apple Pay, you can start making purchases.
- To pay, start by double-tapping your phone's side button.
- Take your iPhone next to the payment machine and keep holding it until the successful payment memo appears.

Delete a Card

You can delete the card(s) you don't wish to use anymore.

- Head to the Wallets app.
- Follow up by tapping the card you intend to remove.

- After this, select ⊙ or ⓘ .
- Now, select "**Remove Card**."

Add Tickets

You can store your digital passes, tickets, vouchers, etc., in the Wallet applications, then show and access them when needed.

- Head to the Wallet app.

- From there, select "**Get**."

- After this, touch "**Find Apps for Wallet**" to install or access the application that connects your wallet to your pass/ticket.

- Follow up by selecting the application that is associated with your ticket/pass, then install or open it.

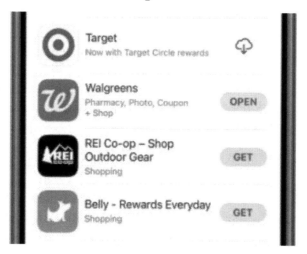

- While in the associated app, select "**Add to Apple Wallet**."

- Afterward, select "**Add**."

Use a Pass

Once you're in a place and needs to verify you pass, do the following:

- Press the ticket/pass notification, then verify using Face ID or passcode. Or double-tap the side key of your iPhone. If these does not work, then launch the Wallet app and select the pass.
- Position your iPhone close to the pass/ticket reader until the checkmark icon shows up on the display or scan with a QR code or barcode.

Share a Pass

You can forward the pass to other people.

- Launch the Wallet app.
- Follow up by selecting the pass/ticket you intend to share.
- Select the Share icon .
- Then select the share method.

Delete a Pass

You can delete a pass that has expired.

- Head to the Wallets app.
- Follow up by tapping the pass you intend to remove.
- After this, select ⋯ or ⓘ .
- Now, select "**Remove Pass**."

Adjust Apple Pay Settings

You can adjust some settings such as double-tapping the Side button to show your tickets and credit cards.

- Launch the Settings app.
- From there, touch "**Wallet & Apple Pay**."
- Follow up by toggling on the "**Double-Click Side Button**" option to make your card(s) and tickets show up

whenever you perform the double-tap action.

Use Apple Cash

Apple Cash enables users to transfer and receive funds in the Wallet application.

Set up Apple Cash
- Head to the Wallet app.
- From there, press the Apple Cash card.
- After that, hit "**Set Up Now.**"

Or,

- Launch the Settings app.
- From there, touch "**Wallet & Apple Pay**."
- Follow up by toggling on "**Apple Cash**."

Tap to Cash

Tap to Cash makes the transfer of funds seamless; all you need to do is bring your phone closer to the recipient's iPhone to send the money.

Enable Bringing Devices Together

Ensure you enable the Bringing Devices Together option on the sender and recipient's phone before you can proceed to send funds.

- Launch the Settings app.
- Then hit "**General.**"
- After this, select "**AirDrop.**"

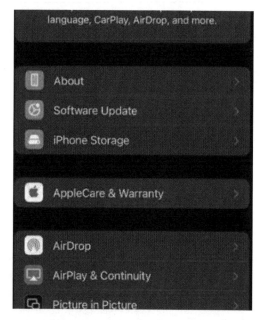

- Proceed by toggling on "**Bringing Devices Together.**"

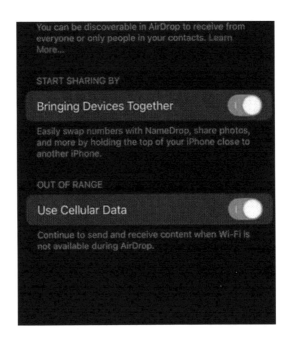

Use Tap to Cash

Ensure you have sufficient funds on your Apple Cash card.

- From the sender's phone, navigate to the Wallet app.
- Then choose your Apple Cash card.

- From there, select "**Send or Request**."

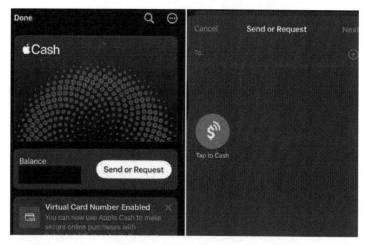

- Next up, hit the "**Tap to Cash**" button.
- Input the amount you want to send.

- Then select "**Next**."
- Follow up by double-tapping the side button to verify the transaction.
- Also, ensure to confirm the transfer using your passcode or Face ID.
- Proceed by placing your iPhone next to the recipient's phone.

The sender will see a memo on their device telling them to stay close to the receiver.

- The receiver will have to select the "**Accept**" button.

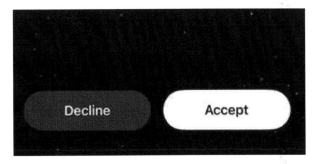

- After a successful deposit, a checkmark will pop up.

Add your Driver's License

Interested users can add their driver's license and state ID to the Wallet application, eliminating the need to carry the physical ID around. Only a few states in the US support the digital license and state identification scheme. So, ensure your state is eligible.

Once you've uploaded your ID, Apple will forward it to the necessary agency in your state for verification.

- Move to the Wallet app.

- From there, select the plus icon.

- Next up, touch **"Driver's License or State ID."**

- Thereafter, select "**Continue.**"

- You'll see a prompt asking you to scan your ID card. Follow up by positioning your ID card in the middle of the camera frame to automatically capture your ID.

- After that, press **"Continue."** If not, hit **"Scan Again"** to rescan the ID.
- Proceed by scanning the back of the ID, then touch **"Continue."** If not, select **"Scan Again"** to rescan it.

- You will be required to show more verification to prove that your identity synchronizes with the information on your driver's ID. Touch "**Continue**" to kickstart this process.
- Touch "**Get Started**" to capture your face.

- Follow the prompts to finish it.

Pay for Transit

You can now pay for your fares using your Apple Pay debit card or the transit card that you've saved in the Wallet application.

Add a Transit Card

- Head to the Wallet app.
- From there, select the plus icon.
- After this, select "**Transit Card**."
- Follow up by selecting a transit card, or find it by using the search field.

Fund your Transit Card

- Launch the Wallet app.
- Follow up by clicking on your transit card.
- Next up, select the More sign ⊙.
- To add money, insert an amount, after that, select "**Add**."

Use Express Transit to Pay for a Ride

Express Transit enables you to pay for your transportation service without using Face ID, unlocking your smartphone, or opening any application.

You can add a default card for Express Transit.

- Head to the Settings app.
- From there, touch "**Wallet & Apple Pay**."
- Next up, hit "**Express Transit Card**."
- It is enabled whenever you include an eligible card.
- Ensure your iPhone is powered on once you're approaching the fare gate or boarding the vehicle.
- Position your phone close to the center of the ticket scanning machine till you hear a vibration.

Pay for Transit

Follow these steps if you are not utilizing Express Transit:

- Ensure your phone is powered on.
- Once you're approaching the fare gate or boarding a vehicle, double-press the side button, then stare at your phone to validate using Face ID, or insert your passcode.
- Follow up by positioning your phone close to the center of the ticket scanning machine till you hear a vibration.

Chapter Four

How to use Apple Intelligence

Apple has integrated its intelligence tool to the iPhone, users can now perform AI tasks.

Use the Clean Up Tool

The Clean Up tool allows photo enthusiasts to crop out unwanted items, people, landmarks, etc., from their images.

- Launch the Photos app.
- Go to the image you wish to edit.
- From there, select the Edit icon from the lower center toolbar.

- After that, press the Clean Up tool at the bottom.

- Follow up by using your finger to circle, click or brush the item you wish to eliminate from the image.
- Hold on while Apple Intelligence removes the chosen item from the image. Select "**Done**" at the upper-right edge to save the modifications.

Summarize Webpages in Safari

Thanks to the integration of Apple Intelligence into the iPhone, users can now use features such as Summarize, Rewrite, Concise, etc., to summarize, paraphrase, and shrink a long text, among other things, while surfing the internet with Safari, Messaging, or the Notes app.

- Head to the Safari app.
- Navigate to the webpage you wish to summarize.
- From there, select the Reader button on the address field.

- After this, select the Show Reader icon from the pop-up menu.

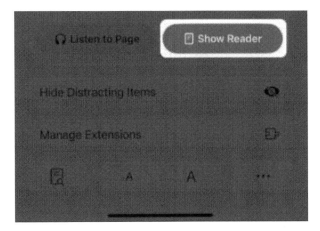

- Afterward, select the Summarize button.

- After Apple's AI scans through the text, you'll see the page summary beneath the page title.
- You can close the Reader mode by

tapping the Reader button ▢ in the address field, then select the Hide icon.

Disable Apple Intelligence in Mail App

You can disable Apple Intelligence if you have no need for it.

- Head to the Settings app.
- From there, touch **"Apple Intelligence & Siri."**

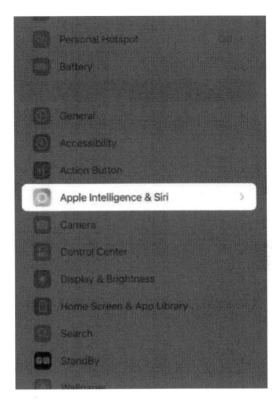

- Finish up by pressing the toggle next to "**Apple Intelligence**."

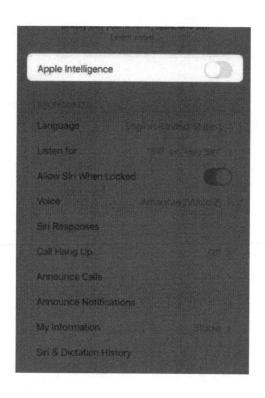

Use Writing Tools

Once you've enabled Apple Intelligence, you can start summarizing, rewriting blog posts, messages, etc.

- Begin by double-tapping on a text to select it.
- You'll see the "**Format**," "**Cut**," "**Copy**." Then select the icon ">" from the pop-up menu.
- Lastly, select "**Writing Tools**."

Use Proofread

You can use the Proofread option to remove typos from your writing.

- After clicking on "**Writing Tools**," one of the options is "**Proofread**." It helps users discover errors, such as misspelled words, wrong punctuation, typos, etc., in their text.

- To view the changes, press the down, up, or arrow. If you wish to accept the modification recommended by Apple Intelligence, then select "**Done**." Or select "**Use Original**" to skip the changes made by Apple AI.

Rewrite Text

The Rewrite tool allows you to paraphrase your chosen text.

- Start by double-tapping to select the text, then drag the handle to select all the words.
- Then select the icon ">" from the pop-up menu.
- Afterward, choose "**Writing Tools**."
- After this, select "**Rewrite**."

Concise the Text

The Concise tool helps to shorten the words, but retains the same meaning.

- Start by double-tapping to select the text, then drag the handle to select all the words.
- Then select the icon ">" from the pop-up menu.
- Afterward, choose "**Writing Tools**."
- After this, select "**Concise**."

Summarize Text

- Start by double-tapping to select the text, then drag the handle to select all the words.
- Then select the icon ">" from the pop-up menu.
- Afterward, choose "**Writing Tools**."
- After this, select "**Summarize**."

Transform Numbers to Tables

The Apple Intelligence tool can also transform your data and numbers into tabular form.

- Start by double-tapping to select the text, then drag the handle to select all the words.
- Then select the icon ">" from the pop-up menu.
- Afterward, choose "**Writing Tools**."
- After this, select "**Table**."

Record Phone Calls

Thanks to Apple Intelligence integration on the iPhone, there's now a call recording feature that allows users to seamlessly record and transcribe all their phone calls.

- Head to the Phone app.

- Then dial a phone number.
- As soon as the call connects, select small Record icon at the upper-left edge of the display.

- The caller and receiver will hear the memo that "This Call Will Be Recorded" to ensure both parties consent to the call recording.

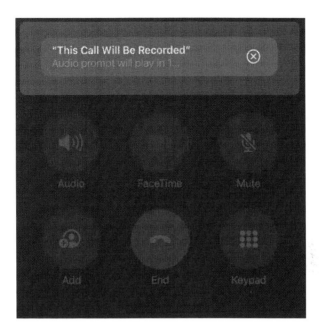

- The recording will be saved in the Notes app.

Listen & Transcribe Phone Calls

After a call drops, you can navigate to the Notes application to listen and see the transcribed version of the call.

- Head to the Notes app.
- From there, select the "**Call Recordings**" folder.

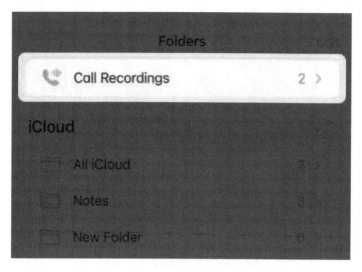

- Follow up by selecting the call recording you wish to hear, then touch the Play button .
- To see the transcribed version of the call, press the call recording. You should see the complete transcription. To avoid reading the entire transcription, select "**Summary**" to view the summary of the recorded call.

Share Call Recordings

You can forward the call recording to another application or move it to another device.

- Head to the Notes app.
- Next, choose the "**Call Recordings**" folder.

- Follow up by choosing the call recording you wish to hear, then touch the Play button.
- Select the three-dot icon at the upper-right edge.

- Choose "**Share Audio**" from the pop-up options.
- Go ahead and choose the application that you wish to share the recorded audio.
- Or, touch the "**Save Audio to Files**" option, then follow the prompts to have it saved to the Files app.

Create a Genmoji

Apple Intelligence also allows users to create a genmoji, which is a personalized emoji that can be created using a text prompt. For example, typing "a beautiful dog donning sunglass" will produce a dog wearing sunglasses.

- Launch the Messages app.

- begin a new message or navigate to an old chat.
- Follow up by writing a prompt in the text box.
- Next up, press the "**Create New Emoji**" prompt to generate the emoji. Hold on to let it generate the emojis.
- Swipe to select your preferred option from the list.
- Hit on "**Insert**" to add the newly generated genmoji to the message.

How to use Music Haptics

Apple created the Music Haptics feature for people with hearing impairments. It allowed them to experience and feel the song in a tactile way.

Turning on Music Haptics causes your phone to gently vibrate in time with the song, allowing you to feel the beat on your palm.

Enable Music Haptics
- Launch the Settings app.
- Move down and select "**Accessibility**."
- Underneath the "**Hearing**" header, press "**Music Haptics**."

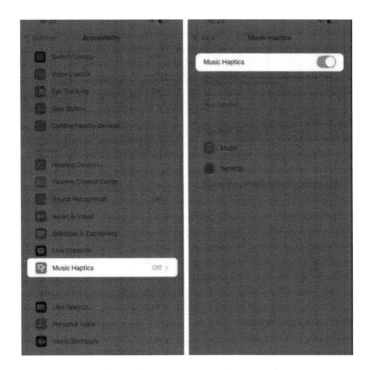

- Finish up by pressing the toggle next to "**Music Haptics**."
- Choose "**Play Sample**" to experience how it works.

After turning on Music Haptics, you'll be able to enable it from the Control Center, Music application, etc.

Adding Music Haptics to Control Center

You can include the Music Haptics shortcut to the Control Center.

- Swipe downward from the upper right edge of your phone to show the Control Center.
- Hit the plus button at the upper left to show the editing mode.
- From there, select "**Add a Control**."
- After this, select "**Music Haptics**" underneath the "**Hearing Accessibility**" header.

Use Music Haptics

Once you're set to see how the Music Haptics functions while playing a song, then head to the Music app.

Hit the Play button to start listening to the song. You'll start to feel the beat through the haptic vibration. The Music Haptics indicator will show underneath the progress bar.

Chapter Five

Eye Tracking

Eye Tracking is an accessibility feature that enables users with motor limitations to use their eyes to do things like open an app, capture screenshots, tap the screen, lock the iPhone, navigate to different pages on a website, and more.

Enable Eye Tracking

Before you're able to use Eye Tracking, you'll have to turn it on and calibrate it.

- Head to the Settings app.
- From there, select "**Accessibility**."

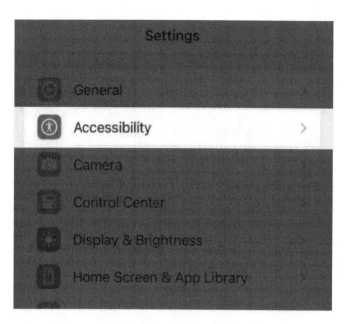

- Then select "**Eye Tracking**."

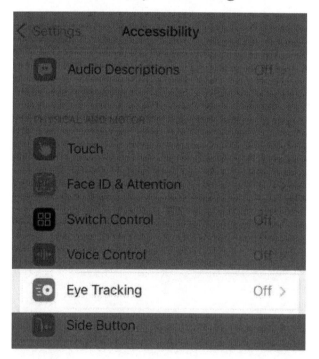

- Ensure your iPhone is about forty-five centimetre from your face.
- Press the switch next to "**Eye Tracking**" to start calibrating the feature.

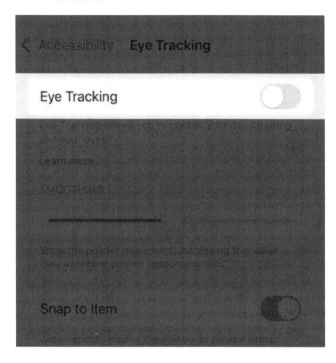

- Proceed by looking at the 10 colouring dots that pops up on your screen.

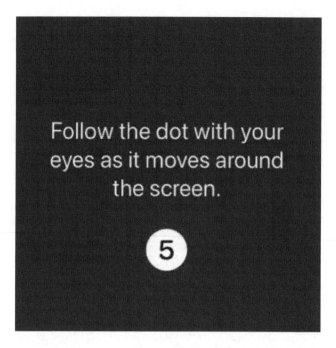

Follow the dot with your eyes as it moves around the screen.

5

- Once you see the dialog, choose **"Yes."**

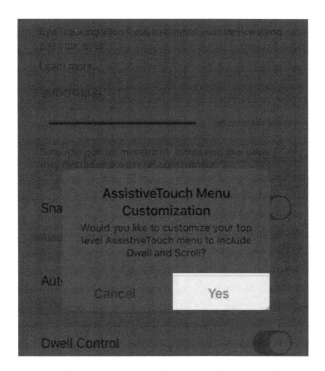

- Follow up by sliding the "**Smoothing**"
  slider to the left to decrease the jerky
  movement of the cursor.

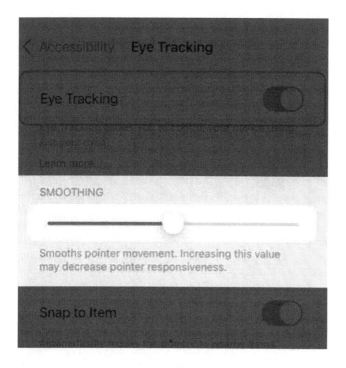

Use Eye Tracking

After you've enabled Eye Tracking, you should see a grey dot marker pop up on the screen. Begin by looking at the screen to control the pointer using your eyes, and choose your preferred option with "**Dwell Control**." Once the pointer is on the appropriate option, keep looking at it for some seconds to open a menu and enable or disable a feature.

You can adjust the duration it takes to execute an action when using Dwell Control.

- Launch the Settings app.
- From there, select "**Accessibility**."

- Next up, hit "**AssistiveTouch**."
- After this, hit "**Dwell Control**."
- Hit on "**Seconds**," then choose an option.

Manage Vehicle Motion Cues

Apple introduced Vehicle Motion Cues to help users reduce motion sickness while traveling in a moving vehicle.

Some users have had issues with what they're feeling and seeing on their phone screen when traveling in a car. When vehicle motion cues are enabled, animated dots will appear in the corner of the phone display.

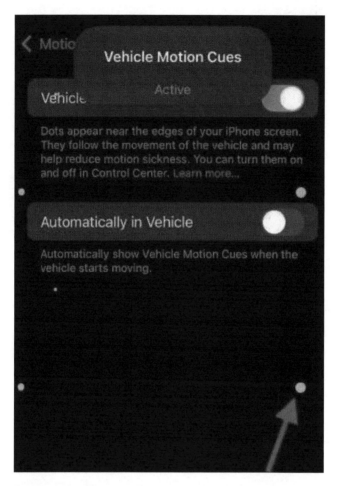

The dots indicate adjustments in the car's motion; this is to ensure that the user doesn't experience motion sickness and helps them to concentrate more on their phone. This is made possible by the in-built sensors of the iPhone that are able to detect a change in motion.

Enable Vehicle Motion Cues

- Launch the Settings app.
- Next up, hit "**Accessibility**."

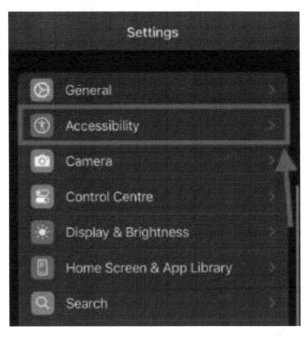

- Then select "**Motion**" underneath the "**Vision section**" heading.

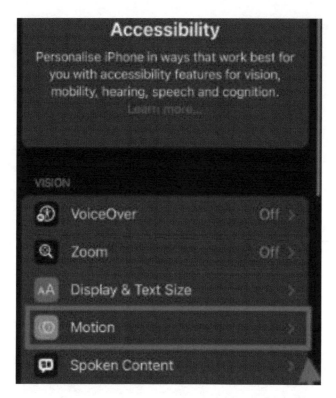

- Select and press the switch next to the **"Show Vehicle Motion Cues"** option to activate it.

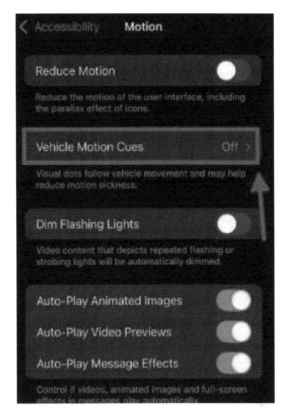

- Whenever you are in a moving car, the feature will automatically enable.

Use Vehicle Motion Cues

You can add the Vehicle Motion Cues icon to the Control Center for swift access.

- Begin by swiping downward from the upper right edge of your phone to show the Control Center.
- Select the plus icon at the upper left.

95

- From there, hit the "**Add a Control**" option in the lower middle.

- Swipe to find, then select the "**Vehicle Motion Cues**" shortcut to include it in the Control Center.

- Follow up by tapping the "**Vehicle Motion Cues**" shortcut, then pick your preferred option from the context menu.

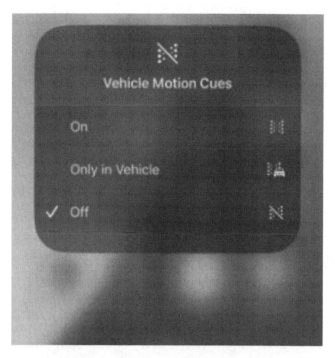

- The "**Only in Vehicle**" option means
  that it'll only activate when you are
  inside a moving car, while "**On**"
  indicates it will be activated all the time.

Use Safari's Distraction

Control Feature

When using Safari to surf a webpage, you can
hide cookie pop-ups, banners, ads, etc.

Enable Distraction Control

- Launch the Safari app.
- Navigate to the webpage where you wish to hide the banners, ads, etc.
- Hit on the Reader icon next to the address bar.

- From there, select "**Hide Distracting Items**."

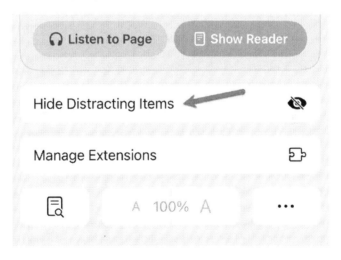

- A memo will pop up, select "**OK**."

Hide Distracting Items

Hiding distracting items will not permanently remove ads and other content that update frequently.

OK

- Follow up by selecting the items you intend to hide on the page.
- A border will appear over it, select "**Hide**" to make the selected item go away.

We and our partners store and/or access information on a device, such as cookies and process personal data, such as unique identifiers and standard information sent by a device for personalised advertising and content, advertising and content measurement, audience research and services development. With your permission we and our partners may use precise geolocation data and identification through device scanning. You may click to consent to our and our 1420 partners' processing as described above. Alternatively you may access

Hide

- Then select "**Done**."

Cancel   1 item hidden   Done

Unhide Items in Safari

If you have no need to hide the item anymore, you can bring it back to the page.

- Select the Reader icon next to the address bar.

- Then select "**Show Hidden Items.**"

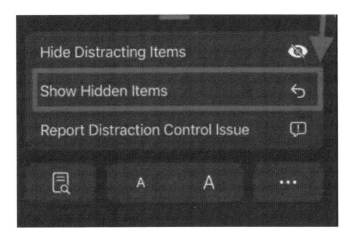

Enable RCS Messaging

RCS, also known as Rich Communication Services, provides iPhone owners with an interactive and dynamic messaging experience. It has features like audio messages, read receipts, emojis, etc.

- Head to the Settings app.
- Move down, then click "**Apps**."
- From there, hit "**Messages**."
- Press the switch next to "**RCS Messaging**" underneath the "**Text Messaging**" section to enable it.

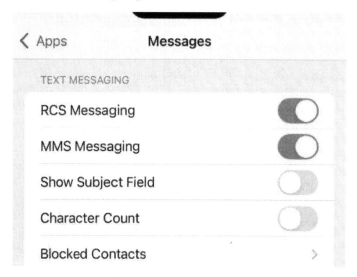

Schedule Text Messages

Thanks to the "**Send Later**" option in the Message application, users can compose a message now and have it automatically delivered at a pre-set time.

- Launch the Messages app.
- Navigate to an existing or start a new message.
- Follow up by composing the Message you wish to schedule.

- After that, choose the plus icon 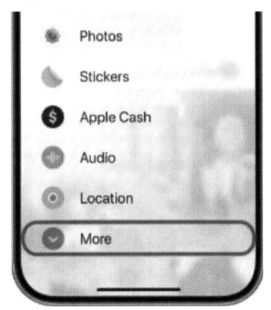 .
- Then choose "**More**" from the pop-up options.

- Then select "**Send later.**"

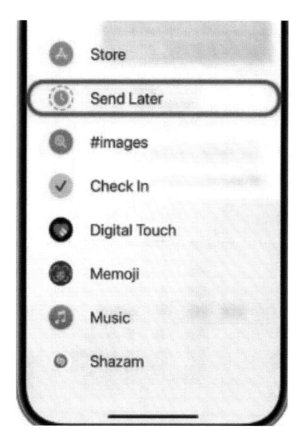

- Proceed by selecting your desired Time and Date.
- After you're done, select the Send button beside the composed text.
- The scheduled message will pop up on your phone screen with the Send Later label that contains the time and date.
- To modify the message, select the Edit button.

Chapter Six

Manage Vibration

Vibration lets your phone discreetly inform you about a notification.

Enable Vibration

- Head to the Settings app.
- From there, touch "**Sounds & Haptics.**"

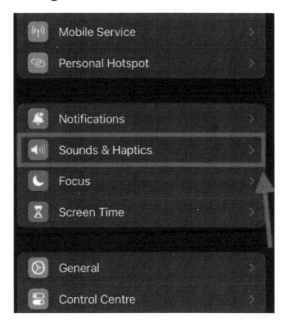

- After that, select "**Haptics**."

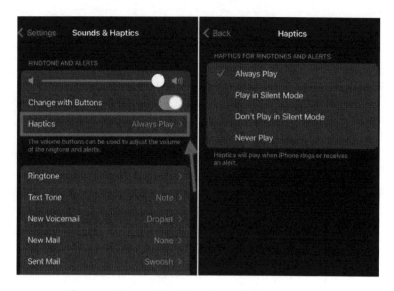

- Choose from the listed option.
- To ensure vibration is enabled every time, select "**Always Play**."
- To disable vibration for all notifications, hit "**Never Play**."

Disable All Vibrations

You can deactivate vibration for all types of notifications including emergencies.

- Move to the Settings app.
- Next up, select "**Accessibility**."

- After this, choose "**Touch.**"

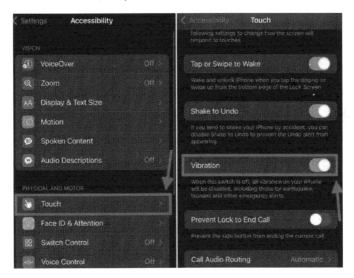

- Press the switch next to "**Vibration**" to deactivate it.

Disable Typing Vibration

You can also deactivate vibration for typing so that your keypad doesn't give haptic feedback.

- Head to the Settings app.
- From there, touch "**Sounds & Haptics**."
- Move down, then select "**Keyboard Feedback**."

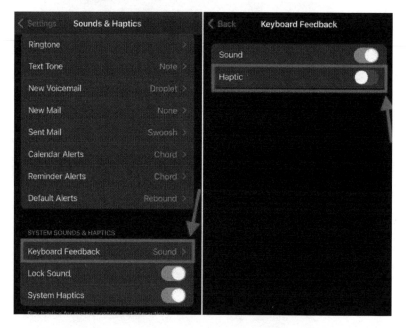

- Press the switch next to "**Haptic**" to deactivate it.
- To disable sound when typing, toggle off the "**Sound**" button.

Activate Dark Mode

If you're in a low-light area and find your iPhone's bright screen causing eye strain, you can activate Dark Mode to adjust the brightness to a level that is comfortable for your eyes.

- Move to the Settings app.
- From there, touch "**Display & Brightness**."

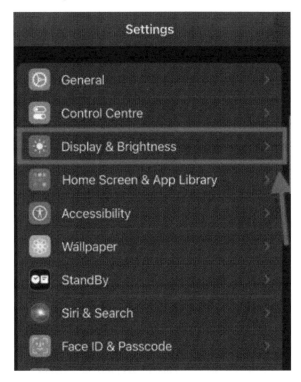

- Press the "**Dark**" checkbox below the "**Appearance**" header.

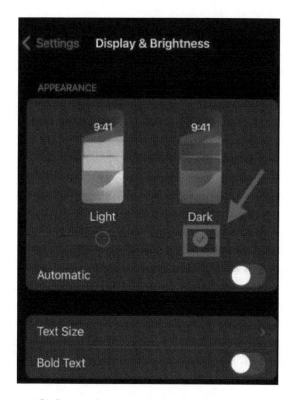

- Click on the "**Light**" checkbox to deactivate Dark Mode.

Customize the Control Center

Control Center is a quick menu to let you enable or disable a feature; Apple has redesigned it. Previously, you'd only modify it via the Settings app. However, you'll now be able to include and remove an icon directly from the Control Center menu. There's also a power icon that lets you power off your phone.

Add Controls to the Control Center

You can include more icons to the Control Center.

- Ensure you're on the Home or Lock Screen, then swipe downward from the upper-right edge to bring up the Control Center.
- Swipe to access more icons such as Music, etc.
- To add more icons, select the plus icon at the upper left of the menu. Or, long-tap an empty area.

- From there, press "**Add a Control**."

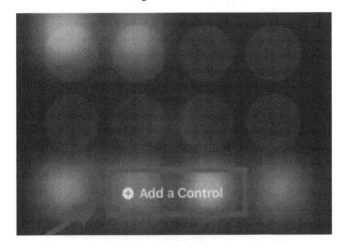

- The Controls menu containing different control icons will appear. Swipe or type into the "**Search**" field to locate a particular control.

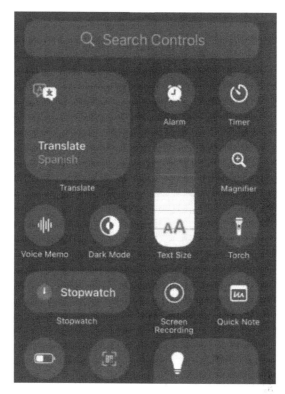

- Once you find the control, click it to have it added to the Control Center.

Reorder & Resize Controls

After adding a control icon, you can adjust the size by long-tapping and dragging the edges.

- Swipe downward from the upper-right edge to bring up the Control Center.
- Select the plus icon to switch to the Edit mode.

- Proceed by holding and dragging the edges of a control icon to increase or reduce the size.

- To reorder the control icon, long-tap it and drag it to your preferred spot on the Control Center.

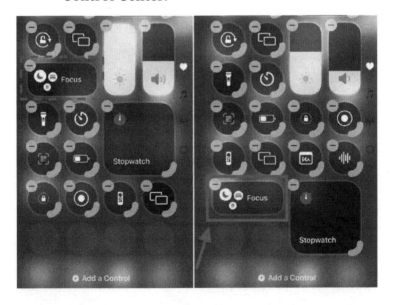

Adding a New Page to Control Center

You can have different control screens so that when you swipe vertically on the Control Center menu, you can see more control icons.

- Navigate to the Control Center menu.
- Select the plus icon or long-tap an empty area to bring up the Edit mode.
- Proceed by selecting the dotted circle underneath the Connectivity icon. The Control Center will now create a new and empty menu.

- Hit on "**Add a Control**," then go ahead and start adding control icons to the new page.

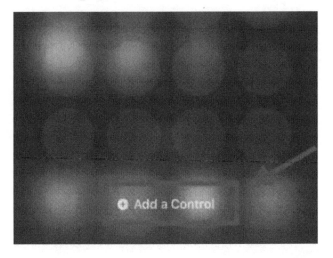

Chapter Seven

Customize your Home Screen

Previously, personalizing the home screen was challenging for users, but iOS 18 has made it easier. You can now make your home screen more visually appealing and intuitive by tweaking it to your preferences. You can adjust the color theme, icon size, add widgets, etc.

Remove App Labels

You can get rid of the app labels (app name) that appears under an application icon.

- Long-tap the background of your phone to initiate the jiggle mode, your applications will start shaking.
- Then select "**Edit**" from the upper left edge.
- Next, select "**Customize**."
- After that, hit "**Large**." You'll find it in the menu at the bottom of the display.

- At this point, your applications will now get bigger.
- To switch to the previous settings, follow the steps above and choose the "**Small**" option.

Change the Color of App Icons

You can adjust the color of your application icons and even give the applications a darker background.

- Long-tap the background of your phone to initiate the jiggle mode, your applications will start shaking.
- Now, press "**Edit**" from the upper left edge.
- Up next, select "**Customize**."
- Next, select the "**Tinted**" button.

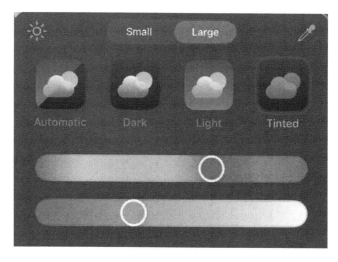

- You'll see a gradient scale pop up at the bottom. Go ahead and slide it to apply your preferred color.
- You can click the eyedropper button at the upper right edge of the window to choose a background color that matches the icons.

To add a darker background to the applications, do this:

- Long-tap the background of your phone to initiate the jiggle mode, your applications will start shaking.
- Now, press "**Edit**" from the upper left edge.
- Up next, select "**Customize**."
- From there, select the "**Dark**" button.
- This option will darken both your phone background and applications especially Apple native apps.

- To make sure the hue matches the wallpaper and background color, hit "**Automatic**."

Darken the Background

If your application icons are too bright or tinted, you can make your phone background darker to make them stand out more.

- Long-tap the background of your phone to initiate the jiggle mode, your applications will start shaking.
- Now, press "**Edit**" from the upper left edge.
- Afterward, select "**Customize**."
- Select the sun icon at the upper left edge of the menu.

Adding a Widget

An app widget provides additional information such as weather forecast, news briefings, soccer results, etc.

- Long-tap the background of your Home screen to initiate the jiggle mode, your applications will start shaking.
- Now, press "**Edit**" from the upper left edge.
- Afterward, select "**Add Widget**."

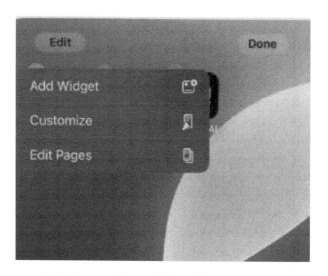

- Follow up by swiping downward to view the available widgets.

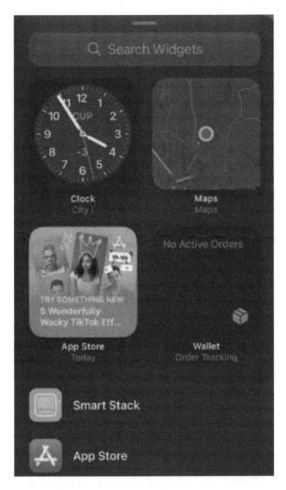

- Select the widget you wish to add.
- Proceed by dragging it to your preferred spot.
- When you're finished, select "**Done.**"

Edit the Home screens

You create multiple Home screens, reorder the icons, and make certain applications appear on them.

- Long-tap an empty space on your Home screen.
- From there, select "**Edit**" from the upper left edge.
- Afterward, hit "**Edit Pages**."
- Go ahead and press the circle to mark the page you intend to see. Press the checkmark for the page you do not intend to see.
- You can reorder the pages by dragging and dropping them to your new preferred spot.
- Afterwards, select "**Done**." Your device will now apply the new layout.

Change an App into a Widget

You can transform an application into a widget. However, it may not work for all apps.

- Long-tap an app. You'll see about four tiny layout buttons pop up in the menu.
- If you select the first button, the application will remain as a normal icon, while the second button will transform it into a small square widget. The third button will transform it into a larger rectangular widget, and the fourth

button will transform it into a larger square widget.

Reorder the Icons

You can change the position of an app icon.

- Long-tap an app icon.
- Next up, hit **"Edit Home Screen."**

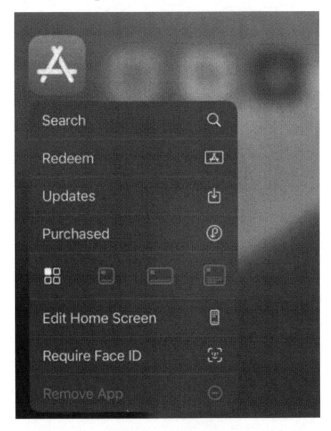

- Follow up by dragging and dropping the icon to your preferred spot.
- Select **"Done"** when you're finished.

Replace Lock Screen Icons

iPhone users can get rid of the camera and flashlight shortcut icons from their lock screen and even substitute them with another shortcut icon.

- Long-tap the Lock Screen.
- Then select "**Customize**."

- Up next, hit "**Lock Screen**."
- Select the minus icon next to the Camera and Flashlight button to remove them.
- To add new shortcut icons, select the plus icon that appears after removing Camera and Flashlight button.
- When finished, hit "**Done**."

Chapter Eight

Use the iPhone Mirroring on Mac

You can make your iPhone screen appear on your Mac and then use it to navigate, open, and view your phone settings, alerts, and other things.

Ensure your Mac has macOS Sequoia installed.

Ensure both devices are logged into the same Apple ID and have 2FA (two-factor authentication) turned on.

Ensure your iPhone is locked and both devices are close to each other.

Then ensure that Bluetooth and Wi-Fi are toggled on for both devices.

Activate iPhone Mirroring in Mac

- Select the iPhone Mirroring app on your Mac.
- Then select "**Continue**."
- Proceed by unlocking your phone.
- From your Mac, hit "**Get Started**."

- An authentication prompt will appear requesting for your Mac password.
- To automatically verify, select "**Authenticate Automatically**." To do this every time you wish to mirror your iPhone, select "**Ask Every Time**."

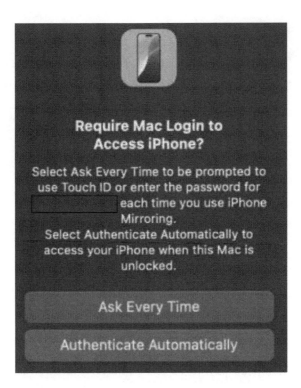

- Your iPhone screen will now pop up on your Mac.
- The **"iPhone in Use"** memo will pop up on your iPhone.

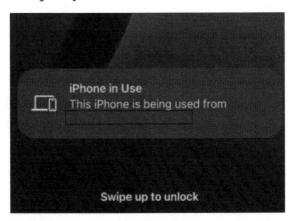

- You can now start using and accessing your iPhone apps on your Mac.

Use iPhone Mirroring

- Once your iPhone content starts showing on your Mac screen, use your Mac trackpad to tap an icon to open it.
- Swipe around or horizontally to navigate your phone Home screen.
- You can switch the iPhone Home Screen from anywhere by tapping the app button at the upper right edge or switcher icon to see a recently opened app.

- Select the Search button to utilize the Spotlight search.

- Thanks to iPhone mirroring, users can use their Mac keyboard to compose notes, emails and other file type on their iPhone.
- Your iPhone notifications will also display on your Mac.

End iPhone Mirroring

You can discontinue your iPhone from mirroring on your Mac.

- On your Mac, select the "**iPhone Mirroring**" button.

- From there, press "**Quit iPhone Mirroring**."
- the mirroring will automatically discontinue once you unlock the iPhone.
- You'll see a prompt to try again. If you're ready to resume mirroring, lock your iPhone, then select the "**Try Again**" button.

Remove Mac from Mirroring List

You can remove your Mac from mirroring your phone.

- Launch the Settings app.
- Then select "**General**."

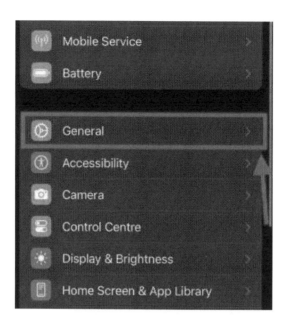

- From there, touch "**AirPlay & Continuity**."

- After this, select **"iPhone Mirroring."**

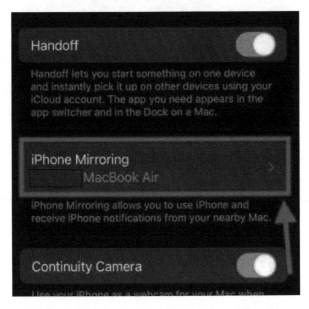

- Follow up by swiping left on the Mac.
- Next, touch the **"Delete"** button.

Chapter Nine

Customize the Photos App

iOS 18 has given the Photos application a revamp. There are no more different tabs; your photos, such as memories, pinned collections, and albums, all appear in one screen view.

Edit the App View

You can personalize the appearance of the Photos app to your liking.

- Head to the Photos app.
- Move down, then hit "**Customize & Reorder**."

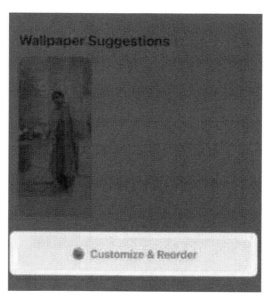

- From there, select the Replace icon (three-dash icon) underneath an Album tile to substitute it with a different one.

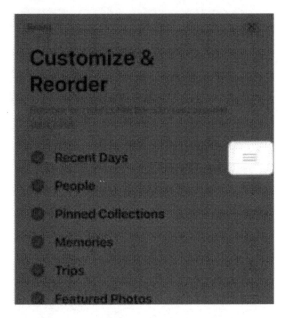

- Follow up by long-tapping and dragging a Collection to adjust its position.

- Or, you can uncheck the collections you wish to delete from the "**Customize & Reorder**" main screen.

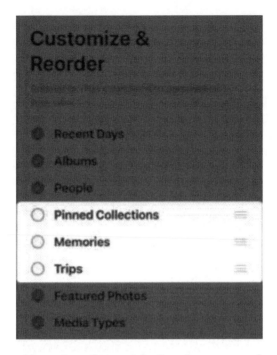

- If you're okay with the changes, select the **X** button in the upper right edge to exit the menu.

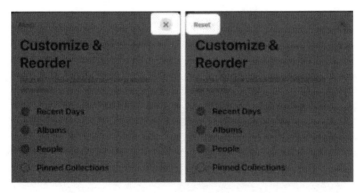

- If you don't like the changes, select the "**Reset**" button in the upper left edge to return the Photos application to default view.

Hide people in the People Section

You'll notice that the People and Pets menu displays the spinning view of photos with a portrait of yourself and others identified by facial recognition. You can customize this section.

To Hide People:

- Navigate to the Photos app.
- Move down, then select "**People**."
- Follow up by choosing the People you wish to hide.
- Then select the three-dot icon in the lower right edge.
- Next up, hit "**Hide**."
- From there, hit "**Remove from People Album**."
- To ensure that the images of the chosen individuals display in one album, hit "**Create New Group**."

You can include new people to the "People & Pets" header. Here's how:

- Select the "**Add People**" option in the lower middle.
- Choose the People.
- Then select "**Add**" from the upper right edge.

Edit Pinned Collections

The "**Pinned Collections**" section contains albums that your device deems important to you. However, you can customize this section to your preference.

- Head to the Photos app.
- Move to the "**Pinned Collection**."

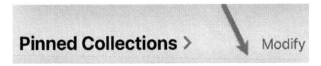

- From there, select the "**Modify**" option.
- To have an album removed from the Pinned Collection, press the minus icon next to the album.

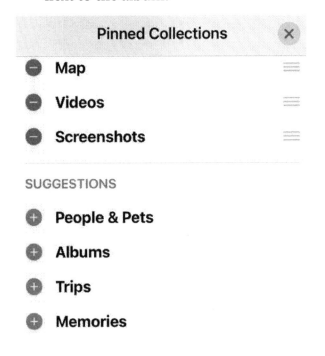

- Or, select the plus icon next to an album to have it added to the Pinned Collection.
- To include a different collection that is not part of the recommended ones, hit on "**Add Collection or Album**."

⊕ Imports

⊕ **Any Collection or Album**

Remove Images from Featured Photos

The iPhone adds photographs of you and others from previous years to the "**Feature Photos**." You can delete images if you prefer not to have them appear there.

- Launch the Photos app.
- Move down, then select "**Featured Photos**."
- From there, choose "**Select**."
- Follow up by choosing the images you wish to get rid of from Featured Photos.
- Next up, select the three dots icon in the lower right edge.
- After this, hit "**Remove from Featured Photos**."

Merge Duplicate Pictures

Apple makes it simple to merge multiple images through the Merge feature which retains the image with the best quality.

- Move to the Photos app.

- Swipe to the "**Utilities**" heading, then press "**Duplicates**."

Utilities

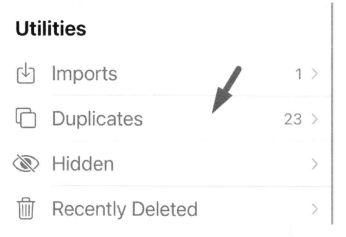

- From there, touch the "**Select**" button to individually select the duplicate photographs.

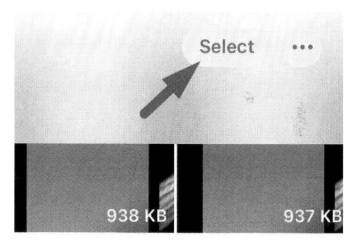

- Or, hit "**Select All**" to highlight the whole duplicate images.

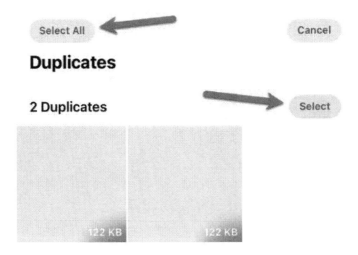

- Then, select the "**Merge**" button.

- Select the "**Merge [number] Exact Copies**."

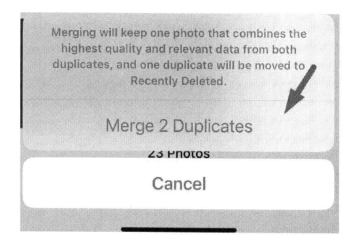

Merging will keep one photo that combines the highest quality and relevant data from both duplicates, and one duplicate will be moved to Recently Deleted.

Merge 2 Duplicates

23 Photos

Cancel

- If you prefer to delete rather than merging them, press the trash button.

23 Photos

Merge (2)

147

Chapter Ten

Use Live Transcripts in Voice Memos

Thanks to iOS 18, users can now generate transcripts for Voice Memos.

You can see the transcript by selecting the Transcript button at the lower left of the menu.

Generate a Live Transcript

You can get a real-time transcript of your recording. Here's how:

- Launch the Voice Memos app.
- Next, select the Record button to begin a recording.

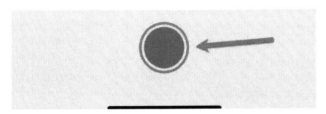

- Follow up by swiping on the recording interface to enlarge the window.

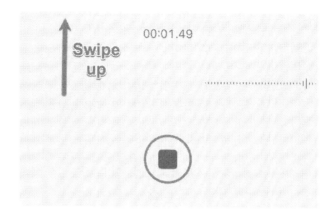

- From there, select the Transcript button (the icon that has quotation marks) at the lower-left to see the real-time transcription.

- You'll see the pop up as you record.

Generate Transcripts for Old Recordings

You can also get the transcript for a recording you've previously done.

149

- Launch the Voice Memos app.
- Navigate to the previous recoding that you wish to get its transcription.
- Click on it to view more options.
- Next up, select the Waveform button.

0:00   –1:00

- From there, select the Transcript button to generate the transcript.

REPLACE   Done

View a Transcript

You'll see the transcript icon next to a recording with transcription.

- Launch the Voice Memos app.
- Select the recording that you wish to view its transcript.

- Next, select the three-dot icon that pops up.

- From there, select the "**View Transcript**" option. You can select the "**Copy transcript**" button to copy and paste it somewhere.

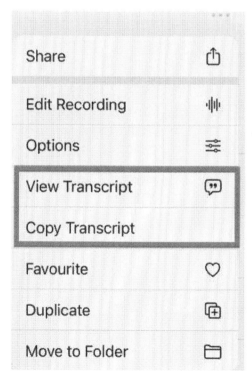

- Click on a word in the transcript to move there in the recording.
- You can find a word, phrase or anything or the transcript by swiping up on the transcript interface and selecting the "**Search**" button.

Live Audio Transcription in Notes

You can also get real-time transcription for your audio in the Notes application.

Use Live Audio Transcript in Notes

- Launch the Notes app.
- Go ahead and begin a new note or navigate to an old one.
- From there, select the Attachment icon.

- Up next, choose "**Record Audio**." You'll now see the recording interface.

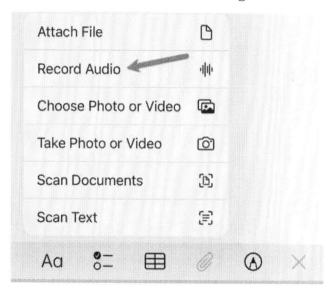

- Choose the "Transcript" icon in the lower-left to get a real-time transcription once you begin the recording, then select the record button to commence your recording.

- After you've completed recording, hit "**Done**."
- A snippet of the transcription will also pop up under the recording in the note. Select it to see the recording when needed.
- From there, select the three-dot icon ⋯
.
- Go ahead and select an option to copy, save as audio or perform another action.

Use Live Captions

Live Caption provides live transcription of audio on your iPhone.

Enable Live Captions

- Move to the Settings app.
- From there, touch "**Accessibility**."

- Beneath the "**Hearing**" heading, touch "**Live Captions**."

155

- Touch the switch beside the "**Live Captions**" button to activate it.

156

Change Live Captions Appearance

You can adjust the appearance of the Live Captions menu.

- Move to the Settings app.
- From there, touch "**Accessibility**."
- Below the "**Hearing**" heading, touch "**Live Captions**."
- Thereafter, touch "**Appearance**."

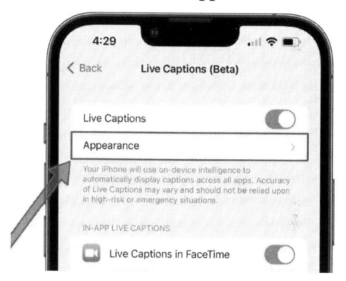

- To make the font bold, touch "**Bold Text**."

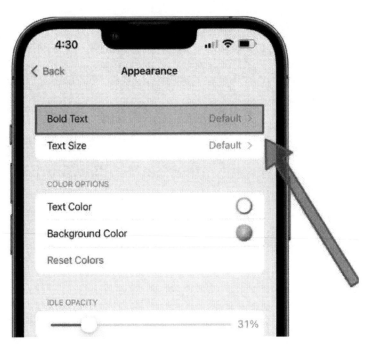

- From there, touch **"On."** Follow up by dragging the slider to adjust the boldness.

- You can also select the "**Text Size**" button on the "**Appearance**" menu to adjust the font.

View Live Captions

Once you've enabled Live Captions, your phone will automatically show the transcription of audio in applications. You can then manage the menu with the buttons.

- Select the Microphone icon to transcribe a dialog near you.

- Select the Maximize icon to expand the transcription interface.

  Select the Minimize icon to switch to a small interface.

- Select the Pause icon to pause the live transcription.
- You can hide the interface by tapping the Collapse icon . Then select the Unhide icon to reveal it.

Use AssistiveTouch

The AssistiveTouch menu contains shortcut to reboot your phone, turn on Blueetooth, Wi-Fi, etc.

Enable AssistiveTouch

- Launch the Settings app.
- From there, touch "**Accessibility**."

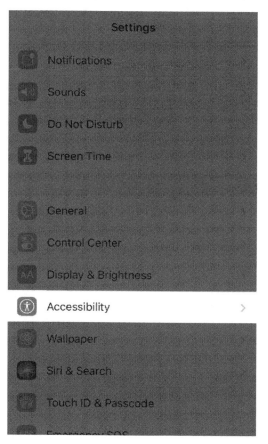

- After that, press **"Touch."**

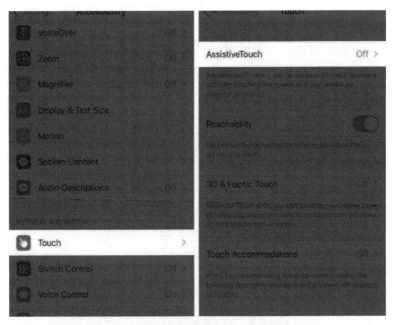

- Thereafter, press **"AssistiveTouch."**

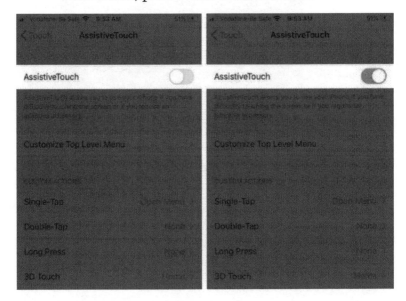

- Touch the toggle beside the "**AssistiveTouch**" button to activate it. You'll see a big circular button pop up on your screen, that's the AssistiveTouch button.

- Click the AssistiveTouch button to access it.

Customize AssistiveTouch
You can edit the AssistiveTouch menu

- Move to the Settings app.
- Thereafter, press "**Accessibility**."
- From there, press "**Touch**."
- After which, select "**AssistiveTouch**."

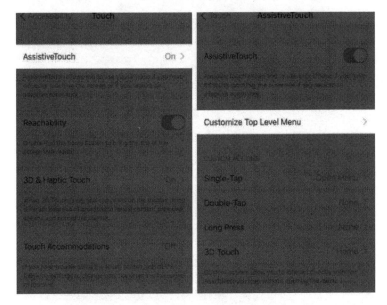

- Up next, touch "**Customize Top Level Menu**."
- Go ahead and choose the button you wish to reassign another function.

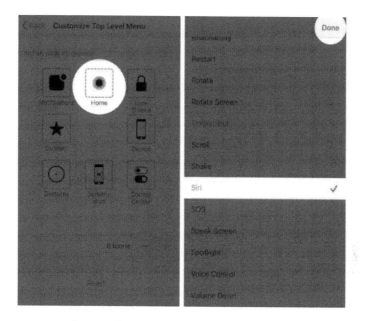

- Then select "**Done**."
- Select the "+" or "-" button to adjust how many icons will show up in the menu.

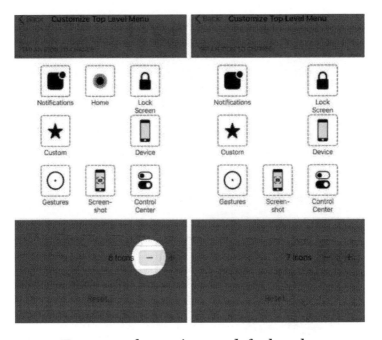

- To return the settings to default, select **"Reset."**

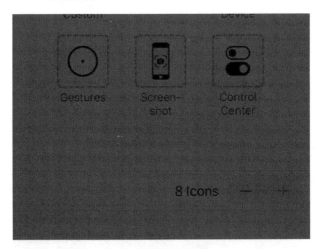

Make New Gestures

You can make your custom gesture and have it saved to the menu.

- Move to the Settings app.
- Thereafter, press "**Accessibility**."
- From there, press "**Touch**."
- After that, select "**AssistiveTouch**."
- Up next, touch "**Create New Gesture**."
- Touch and swipe on the display to begin recording.
- Once done, touch "**Stop**."
- Select "**Play**" to preview the new gesture. To record again, hit "**Record**."
- Afterward, select "**Save**."

Chapter Eleven

Plan Hikes & Other Adventures

The revamped Apple Maps offers hikers and adventurers an improved method of planning their trips. Hikers now have access to a comprehensive map, live data, and user-created content, etc.

Plan a Hike for Known Trailheads

You can make personalized topographical hiking route maps and view them on your device.

- Launch the Apple Maps.
- Follow up by searching for a trail/nature park.
- Then choose the Trailheads/Trail option.
- Next up, select a trail.
- From there, touch **"Plan a Hike."**

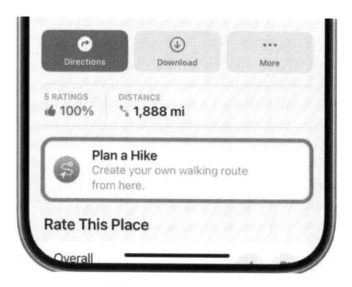

- Proceed by tapping on the map to enter your path.
- You can then see the distance and height.
- Go ahead and select Close Loop, Reverse, etc.
- Finish up by saving and naming the route.
- Lastly, hit "**Done**."

You can begin a personalize route of the park or trail if it doesn't show the "Trailheads" button.

Plan a Custom Route

- Move to the Apple Maps app.
- Locate the "**Library**" section.

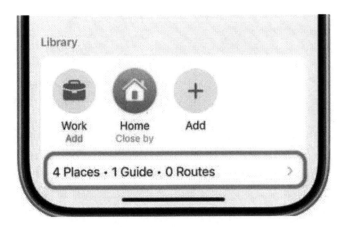

- Proceed by tapping under it to select "Routes," "Places," etc.

- Once you've chosen Routes, next up, select **"Create Route."**

- Follow up by tapping the map to input a start point.
- Go ahead and click other places to go.
- The options such as "Close Loop," "Reverse," etc., will appear.
- Lastly, hit "**Save**."

Use the Calculator App

You can now do complex mathematical calculations and covert different units in the Calculator app.

Use Math Notes

Math Notes let you solve complex equation all thanks to the integration of Apple Intelligence.

- Navigate to the Calculator app.
- Then select the calculator button in the bottom.

- Up next, choose "**Math Notes**." You'll be redirected to the Notes application.

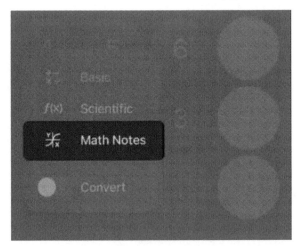

- From there, choose the pen button.

- Proceed by typing the equation and insert the equals sign "=." You'll see the answer immediately.

Use Unit Conversions

You can now get real-time conversion of units, currencies, etc.

- Launch the Calculator app.
- Then select the calculator icon.
- Press the switch beside the "**Convert**" button.

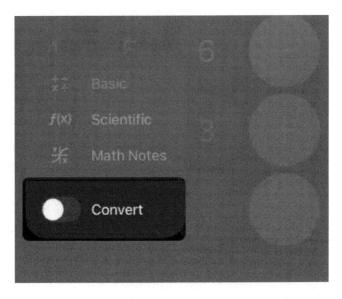

- Click on the unit that appears to the right of the figure on top.
- Proceed by selecting the unit category.
- Then select the unit, and hit "**Done**."
- You can also switch the unit at the bottom.
- Go ahead and input the number you wish to convert.

Use the Journal App

The Journal application lets you reflect and document your daily thoughts, experiences, journeys, moments, trips, memories, and more through audio, videos, and images. The app also offers custom suggestions on things you can write.

Once you open the Journal application, go through the prompts to set it up.

Make a Journal Entry

You can start jotting down your thoughts once you've set up the app.

- Launch the Journal app.

- Then select the Compose icon ⊕.
- Up next, hit "**New Entry**." Alternatively, you can select from the suggestion or prompt.

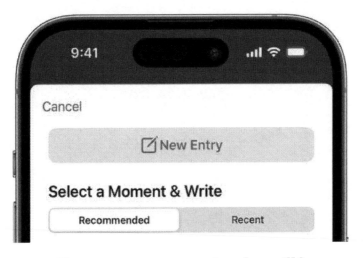

- You can save a suggestion that will be used in future by long-tapping on the suggestion and selecting "**Save Without Writing**."

Use Journaling Suggestions

Journaling suggestions can systematically organize your images, exercises, outings, etc., to enable you to recall and reminisce over your experiences.

- Launch the Journal app.

- Select the Compose icon ⊕.
- Go through the recommended suggestions. Click on "**Recent**" to view the suggestions filtered by time.
- You can begin a fresh entry that comprises the entire suggested attachments by clicking the Compose

icon ⊕ in the lower right edge of the suggestion. Alternately, you can see a snippet of the attachment before making the entry by tapping the suggestion and then swiping across the attachments to explore it.

- You can view more information about the attachment by tapping the List icon ☰ ☰ ☰.

- Then select "**Start Writing**."

- You can remove a suggestion by long-tapping on it and selecting "**Remove**."

Disable Journaling Suggestions

- Launch the Settings app.
- Move down, then select "**Journal**."
- Proceed by toggling off the "**Skip Journaling Suggestions**" option beneath the "**New Entry**" section.

Chapter Twelve

Camera App

One of the big selling points of the iPhone is its ability to capture high-quality and cinematic photos and videos, thereby making your pictures seem like they were taken by a professional.

Take a photo

Once you're ready to capture an image, do this:

- Launch the Camera app.
- Swipe horizontally on the buttons above the Shutter icon to switch to different Camera mode such as Video, Portrait, etc.

- Then select the Shutter button .

Focus and Exposure

Your phone is capable of automatically adjusting the exposure, focus, and face recognition before taking a picture. But you may still tweak them by yourself.

- Head to the Camera app.
- Touch the display to see the focus and exposure window.

- Select the spot where you wish the focus to be.
- You can go ahead to adjust the exposure by dragging up or down the button ☀ next to the focus point.

Camera flash

Although the iPhone is able to automatically enable the camera flash when the lighting condition is low. However, you can still enable it yourself when capturing photos.

- Select the Flash button ⚡ to enable or disable automatic flash.

- Select the Menu button ⌃. From there, select the Flash button to pick an option: "**Auto**," "**On**," or "**Off**."

Adding Filter to a photo

You can adjust the vibrance and hue of an image through filter.

- Head to the Camera app.
- Swipe on the Camera mode selector to switch to the Photo or Portrait mode.

- Choose the Menu button ⌃.

- From there, select 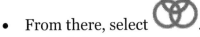.
- Swipe left or right to see the snippet of more filters.
- Select the Shutter button to snap the photo.

Using the Camera timer

Camera timer gives you some seconds before it snaps a photo. You can use it to position appropriately before a shot is taken.

- Head to the Camera app.

- Then select ⌃.

- After that, select ⏱.
- From there, select or "**3s**," or "**10s**."
- Then select the Shutter button to commence the timer.

Shoot a Live Photo

Thanks to Live Photo, users can record the photo, audio, and events before and after the recording.

- Head to the Camera app.

- You'll see the button ⊚ at the top menu, click it.
- Then select the Shutter button to snap a Live Photo.

Add a Photographic Style

With Photographic Style, you can customize the layout and look of the images.

- Head to the Camera app.

- Select the Menu button ⌃.
- Go ahead and select the Styles button ⧉.

- Swipe to see other styles such as "**Cool**," "**Vibrant**," "**Warm**," etc.

- Then select ⧉ to apply the Photographic Style.

- Hit on ⧉ to switch the added Photographic Style.
- To resort to the default, select "**Standard**."

Use Burst mode

Burst mode lets you capture rapidly moving images.

- Move to the Camera app.
- Slide the Shutter button to the left, then let go to discontinue the capture.
- You can pick the photo you wish to retain by tapping on the thumbnail, then choose "**Select**."
- Next, select "**Done**."

Shoot panoramic photos

Thanks to the Panoramic mode, your iPhone camera can shoot images with an extended depth of view.

- Head to the Camera app.
- Swipe on the mode selector to select the Pano mode.
- Next up, select the Shutter button.
- Cautiously pan your camera towards the arrow's direction and ensure you're keep focus on the center line.
- Then select the Shutter button again.
- Select the arrow to pan to the other direction.

Shoot Night mode photos

When the outside light is dim, you can still get a good shot by switching to night mode. Night mode automatically adjusts the exposure, but you have the option to manually tweak it if you prefer.

- Head to the Camera app.
- The moment tour camera notices that it's a low lighting environment, it will turn on Night mode.
- Select the button ⊜ at the top menu to activate or deactivate Night mode.

- You can experiment with it by tapping the button ⌃ , then select the icon ⊜ .
- Then select the Shutter button to capture the image.

Turn on Apple ProRAW

To provide a high-resolution image, Apple ProRAW blends the usual RAW format with their imaging technology.

Ensure you toggle on ProRaw before you can start capturing.

- Move to the Settings app.
- From there, select "**Camera**."
- Then select "**Formats**."
- Finish up by toggling the switch beside the "**ProRAW & Resolution Control**" option.

Shoot with Apple ProRAW

Once you've enabled the ProRaw, you can start capturing images in that format.

- Head to the Camera app.

- From there, hit on the button **RAW MAX** to activate ProRAW.
- Select the Shutter button to capture.
- When you're capturing, you can tap **RAW MAX** or **RAW MAX** to activate or deactivate ProRAW.

Shoot a macro photo or video

Thanks to Macro photo, users can take close-up captures of their target subject or objects, especially smaller objects.

- Head to the Camera app.

- Swipe on the mode selector to choose the "**Photo**" or "**Video**" mode.
- Get within around two centimeters of the subject you want to snap a picture of.
- After that, you may take a picture by clicking the shutter button or start recording a video by clicking the record icon.

Shoot a macro slow-motion or time-lapse video

- Head to the Camera app.
- Swipe on the mode selector to select the "**Time-lapse**" or "**Slo-mo**" mode.
- From there, hit "**.5x**" to toggle on the ultra-wide lens.
- Move close to the subject.
- Then select the Record icon to commence recording.

You'll be able to customize your close-up shots.

- Get close to the subject. Once you are within a macro distance, you'll see the

  button .

- Select the button if you wish to deactivate macro switch.

- You can activate automatic macro by

  tapping the button  .

Shoot portraits

Portrait shots blurs the background and makes the subject stand out.

- Head to the Camera app.
- Follow up by swiping to select the "**Portrait**" mode.
- Ensure the subject you wish to capture appear inside the yellow box.
- Proceed by pinching the screen to zoom.

- Slide the Lighting button  to choose your desired effect.
- Lastly, select the Shutter button.

Adjust Depth Control

You can tweak the level of the blurred background.

- Head to the Camera app.
- Follow up by swiping to select the "**Portrait**" mode.
- Lock on the subject.
- Then select the button  in the top-right edge.

- Go ahead and slide the Depth slider to adjust the effect.
- Next up, select the Shutter button to snap the photograph.

Adjust Portrait Lighting

You'll be able to change the position and level of the lighting.

- Move to the Camera app.
- Select the "**Portrait**" mode.

- Slide the button ![lighting effect button] to select a lighting effect.

- Next, select the button ![lighting adjust button]. Slide the Lighting slider to adjust the effect.

- Lastly, select the Shutter button to capture.

Use Live Text

The Camera application can automatically text and numbers, and you can have them translated, copied, dialed, or searched online.

- Head to the Camera app.
- Position your iPhone so that the text/number will appear within the camera box.
- A yellow box will show on top of the identified text/number.

- Select the button ⌐⌐⌐.
- Next up, hit "Look Up," "Copy," "Translate," or others to carry out your desired action.

- Select the button ⬚ to return to Camera.

Activate HDR video

HDR helps you get the enhanced version of any video captured by your camera.

- Head to the Settings app.
- Next up, select "**Camera**."
- From there, select "**Record Video**."
- Go ahead and toggle on the "**HDR Video**" switch.

Shoot videos in Cinematic mode

Cinematic mode works similarly to portrait mode; it blurs the background and makes the subject stand out when recording video, and you can adjust the level of blur as well.

- Head to the Camera app.
- Select the "**Cinematic mode**."
- Simply pinch in or out to zoom.

- Select the button 𝑓 to adjust the depth-of-field, then move the slider.
- Select the Record button to begin.

Shoot ProRes videos

ProRes videos are enhanced quality with less compression and can be used for professional videos and TV commercials.

Activate ProRes

Ensure you've turned on ProRes in the Settings app before you start shooting. Here's how:

- Head to the Settings app.
- From there, select "**Camera**."
- After this, choose "**Formats**."
- Select the switch beside the "**Apple ProRes**" button to activate it.

Shoot a ProRes video

Once you've activated the Apple ProRes, you can start recording videos in that format.

- Move to the Camera app.
- Then select the "**Video**" mode.
- Next up, select the button 	HD🅁 	to activate ProRes.
- Afterward, select the Record button to commence the video recording.
- Follow up by pinching in or out to zoom.

- Then select the button **ProRes HDR** to deactivate ProRes recording.

Shoot a QuickTake video

To record QuickTake videos, you'll have to switch to the Photo mode. Then slide the Record button to lock the position and keep taking still photographs.

- Head to the Camera app.
- Follow up by long-pressing the Shutter button to commence capturing a QuickTake video.
- Then drag the Shutter button towards the right, then let go for hand-free shooting.
- Underneath the box, the Shutter and Record button will appear. Select the

Shutter button to take a still photograph while recording.

- Hit the Record button once more to end the recording.

Shoot a slow-motion video

- Head to the Camera app.
- Select the "**Slo-mo**" mode.
- Then select the Record button to begin recording.
- You can snap a still photograph while recording by pressing the Shutter button.
- Select the Record button to discontinue the recording.
- You'll be able to make some portion of the video play as slow motion, while the other will play at normal speed. Begin by tapping the video thumbnail.
- Then select "**Edit**."
- Slide the vertical blocks underneath the viewer to selection the portion that will play in slow motion.

Shoot a time-lapse video

- Move to the Camera app.
- Then select "**Time-lapse**" mode.
- Select the Record button to commence recording.

Take a Screenshot

You can capture the current menu or screen on your phone.

- Press the side and volume up buttons at once.

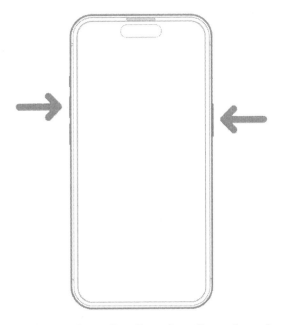

- Then select the thumbnail to view the captured screen.

Use Screen Recording

The iPhone has a built-in tool that can record your screen.

- Swipe downward from the upper right to bring up the Control Center.
- From there, select the Screen Record button to record without audio. To add sound, long-press the screen record button.

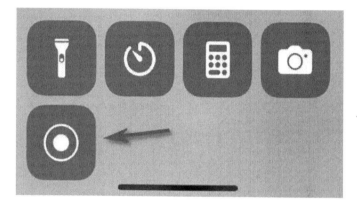

- Up next, touch the microphone button to add audio. Then select "**Start Recording.**"

- Screen recording will begin once the countdown elapses. To discontinue the screen recording, touch the red timer at the upper-left menu. From there, select the "**Stop**" option.

- You'll find the recording in the Photos app.

Enable Audio Playback
While Recording Videos

Thanks to Audio Playback, your audio can still play in the background while you're shooting in video mode on the Camera application.

- Head to the Settings app.

- From there, choose "**Camera**."

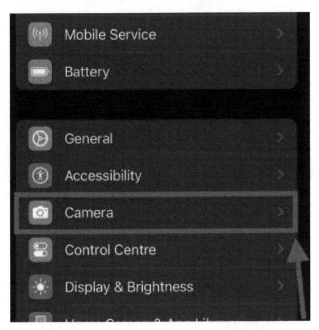

- Up next, select "**Record Sound**."

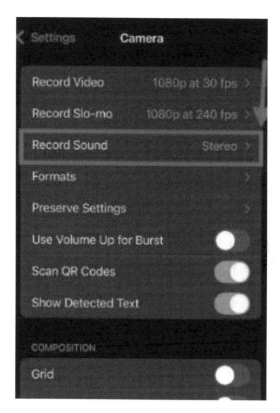

- Press the switch next to "**Allow Audio PlayBack**" to activate it.

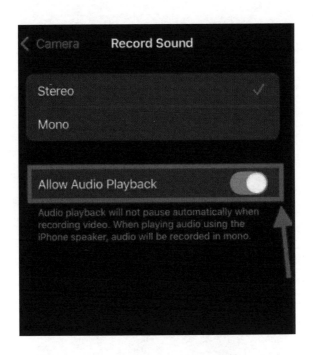

Chapter Thirteen

Use Find My App

With the Find My app, users can track the whereabouts of their friends, loved ones, and their missing devices. They can also remotely lock or erase their device data, preventing a third party from accessing the device content.

Activate Find My

Ensure you enable the Find My iPhone in the Settings app.

- Head to the Settings app.
- Select your Apple ID at the upper menu.
- From there, touch "**Find My**."
- To ensure your loved ones know your location, touch the switch next to "**Share My Location**" to activate it.
- Then select "**Find My iPhone**."

- Ensure you toggle on the "**Find My iPhone**" switch.
- Toggle on "**Find My network**" so that you'll be able to see your missing device when it is also offline.
- Touch the switch beside the "**Send Last Location**" option so that the location of the device will be forwarded to Apple's server once the battery is drained.

Also, ensure you toggle on Location Services. Here's how:

- Launch the Settings app.
- From there, touch "**Privacy & Security**."
- Up next, select "**Location Services**."

- Touch the switch beside the "**Location Services**" button.

Set location sharing

You can now navigate to the Find My app and start customizing the settings so that your location can be shared.

- Head to the Find My app.
- Select the "**Me**" tab.
- Touch the switch next to "**Share My Location**" to activate it.

- In the "**From**," pane, the device sharing your location will appear.

- Ensure you select "**Use This iPhone as My Location.**"

Add a location label

You can add a description for your location.

- Move to the Find My app.
- Select the "**Me**" tab.
- From there, choose "**Location**."
- Follow up by selecting a label. Hit on "**Add Custom Label**" to name a description, then choose "**Done**."

Share your location

If you're going somewhere you're not sure of, you can select a contact(s) that will be aware of your location.

- Head to the Find My app.
- Then select "**People**" tab.

- After that, select the plus button $+$.
- Thereafter, touch "**Share My Location**."

- Choose a contact in the "**To**" pane. Or, select the plus button to select you're your contact list.
- To send your location, select "**Send**," then select how long you will be sharing your location with them.

End sharing your location

You can discontinue sharing of your location with someone.

- Head to the Find My app.
- Then select "**People**" tab.
- Choose the person.
- Up next, touch "**Stop Sharing My Location**."
- From there, press "**Stop Sharing Location**."

Get directions to a friend

If a friend is sharing their location, you can view it on a map.

- Move to the Find My app.
- From there, select the "**People**" tab.
- Select the friend.
- After that, select the "**Directions**" button to view it on a Map.

See your Lost Device

Once you've enabled the Find My iPhone or another gadget, you can access their location. Here's how:

- Head to the Find My app.
- From there, select the "**Devices**" tab.

- Choose the device to see its location on the map.
- Then select an option.

Erase a Lost Device

You'll be able to remotely wipe your data from the device if recovering it becomes impossible.

- Move to the Find My app.
- Select the "**Devices**" tab.
- Then choose the lost device.
- After that, touch "**Erase This Device**."
- Follow the prompts.

Label a Device as Lost

You can label your misplaced device as lost.

- Launch the Find My app.
- From there, hit on the "**Devices**" tab.
- Select the device you wish to tag.
- Beneath the "**Mark As Lost**" card, select "**Activate**."

- Hit on "**Continue**."
- Follow the prompts.

Request to see someone's location

- Launch the Find My app.
- Choose the "**People**" tab.
- Choose the person's location who you wish to view their location.

- If the person doesn't show up, it indicates that you're not sharing your location with them.
- Then hit on "**Ask To Follow Location**."
- Once they accept the request, you'll be able to see their location.

Add AirTag

- Navigate to your phone Home Screen.
- Position the AirTag close to your phone.
- Then select "**Connect**" from your phone screen.
- Follow up by selecting a name or press "**Custom Name**" to input your preferred name and choose an emoji.
- After that, select "**Continue**."
- Go ahead and select "Continue" to have the AirTag registered to your Apple ID.
- Lastly, select "**Finish**."

Or,

- Navigate to the Find My app.

- From there, select the plus button ✛.
- Afterward, select "**Add AirTag**."

Adjust the name/emoji of an AirTag

- Head to the Find My app.

- Select the "**Items**" tab.
- Choose the AirTag that you wish to change its name or emoji.
- Up next, touch "**Rename Item**."
- Follow up by selecting from the list or hit on the "**Custom Name**" button to input a name/emoji.
- Then hit "**Done**."

Activate Lost Mode for an item

You can label your missing Item as lost.

- Head to the Find My app.
- Select the "**Items**" tab.
- Choose the missing item.
- Select the "**Enable**" button underneath "**Lost Mode**."
- Go through the onscreen direction to input your phone number or touch the "Use an email address" button to add your email instead.
- Lastly, select "**Activate**."

Deactivate Lost Mode for an item

Once you've found your item, you can disable the Lost Mode.

- Head to the Find My app.
- Select the "**Items**" tab.
- Choose the item.

- Underneath "**Lost Mode**," select "**Enabled**."
- From there, touch "**Turn Off Lost Mode**."
- Lastly, select "**Turn Off**."

Adding a third-party item

You can third-party items to the Find My app to allow for tracking when it gets missing.

Go through the manufacturer's direction to ensure that the item becomes discoverable.

- Launch the Find My app.
- From there, touch "**Add Other Item**."
- After that, select "**Connect**."
- Follow up by typing a name and choosing an emoji.
- Afterward, select "**Continue**."
- Next up, touch "**Continue**" to have the item added to your Apple ID.
- After this, choose "**Finish**."

Chapter Fourteen

Set up Siri

Siri help you perform quick task such as turning on a feature and scanning the internet for query and these can be done hands-free.

- Launch the Settings app.
- From there, touch "**Siri & Search**."
- Follow up by touching the switch beside the "**Listen for "Hey Siri**" button to activate it.

- Follow the prompts.
- You'll see a prompt, select "**Continue**."
- Follow the prompts.

Enable Bluetooth

- Move to the Settings app.
- From there, touch "**Bluetooth**."
- Toggle on the Bluetooth button.

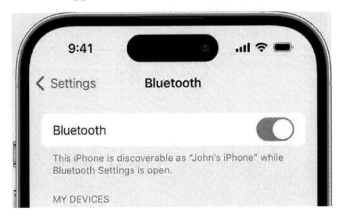

- From the menu, pick the Bluetooth device you wish to pair with.

How to use AirDrop

With AirDrop you can transfer and receive files from other people.

- Navigate to the app where the file is located.

- Select the "**Share**" option or .
- After that, select the "**AirDrop**" button.

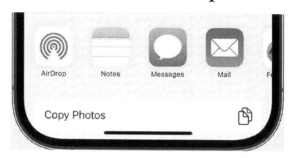

- Then select the receiver.

Accept AirDrop

To accept an AirDrop file, select the "**Accept**" button. Otherwise, select "**Decline**."

Adjust AirDrop settings

You'll be able to customize the people who you can send and receive files from.

- Move to the Settings app.
- From there, select "**General**."
- After that, touch "**AirDrop**."
- To allow AirDrop for contacts only, touch "**Contacts Only**." Or choose the other option.

Enable Emergency Alerts

Apple let you get public emergency alerts on your phone.

- Move to the Settings app.
- From there, touch "**Notifications**."
- Below the "**Government Alerts**" heading, touch the switch beside the "**AMBER Alerts**" button to activate or deactivate it. Do the same for other toggles there.

- Up next, select "**Emergency Alerts**," and toggle it on.

Enable Local Awareness

Residents of the US can enable local awareness to utilize their accurate location to enhance the accuracy and timely delivery of emergency notifications.

- Move to the Settings app.
- After that, select "**Notifications**."
- Then select "**Emergency Alerts**" underneath the "**Government Alerts**" heading.
- Select the switch next to "**Local Awareness**" to activate it.

Use Safety Check

Safety Check let you revoke access from application and persons you're sharing your information with.

Adding Emergency Reset

- Launch the Settings app.
- From there, touch "**Privacy & Security**."
- After that, touch "**Safety Check**."
- Thereafter, choose "**Emergency Reset**."

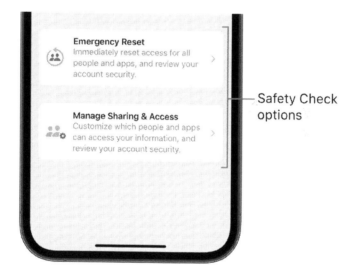

- You maybe be asked to authenticate using Face ID or passcode.
- Up After this, press "**Start Emergency Reset**."

- After this, touch "**Reset People & Apps.**"
- After which, hit "**Reset.**"
- Follow the prompts.

Adding Safety Check

The Manage Sharing & Access menu let you see who has permission and you can revoke it from there.

- Launch the Settings app.
- From there, touch "**Privacy & Security.**"

- After that, touch "**Safety Check**."

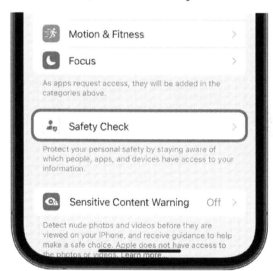

- Thereafter, hit on "**Manage Sharing & Access**."
- Authenticate with your Face ID or Passcode.
- After which, choose "**Continue**."

- Follow the prompts.

Scan your Document

- Launch the Notes app.

- From there, press the pencil button.

- Thereafter, select the camera button .

- Up next, select **Scan Documents** .

- Position your document to be captured by the camera.
- It will automatically scan the document.

  If not, press the shutter button .
- Then choose "**Save**."

Sign your document

You can add signature to a document.

223

- Launch the Notes app.
- Select the document.

- Then choose the Share icon .
- From there, select the Markup button .

- After that, touch the plus icon .

- Up next, select Signature 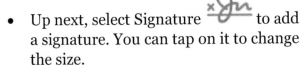 to add a signature. You can tap on it to change the size.
- When finished, touch "**Done**."

Conclusion

You can also refer back to this book whenever you need to look up something. I hope you enjoyed reading this guide and found the instructions useful. Stay tuned for more content.

About the Author

Shawn Blaine is a gadget reviewer, programmer, and computer geek. He has worked for some big tech companies in the past. He's currently focused on coding and blockchain development but still finds time to write and teach people how to use their smart devices to the fullest.

Index

229

Made in the USA
Monee, IL
04 October 2024